Paul
Wellstone

Paul Wellstone

The Life of a
PASSIONATE
PROGRESSIVE

Bill Lofy

THE UNIVERSITY OF MICHIGAN PRESS
Ann Arbor

Copyright © by the University of Michigan 2005
All rights reserved
Published in the United States of America by
The University of Michigan Press
Manufactured in the United States of America
⊛ Printed on acid-free paper

2008   2007   2006   2005   4   3   2   1

A CIP catalog record for this book is available from the British Library.

Library of Congress Cataloging-in-Publication Data

Lofy, Bill.
     Paul Wellstone : the life of a passionate progressive / Bill Lofy.
         p.   cm.
     Includes bibliographical references.
     ISBN-13: 978-0-472-03119-1 (pbk. : alk. paper)
     ISBN-10: 0-472-03119-8 (pbk. : alk. paper)
         1. Wellstone, Paul David.   2. Legislators—United States—Biography.
     3. United States. Congress. Senate—Biography.   4. Progressivism (United
     States politics)   I. Title.

     E840.8.W457L64   2005
     328.73'092—dc22   2005011742

To my mom,
MARY LOFY,
my first political hero

Only he has the calling for politics who is sure that he shall not crumble when the world from his point of view is too stupid or too base for what he has to offer. Only he who in the face of all this can say "In spite of it all!" has the calling for politics.

— Max Weber, *"Politics as a Vocation"*

Contents

Acknowledgments

THIS BOOK WOULD not have been written without the support, advice, and encouragement of Professor Fred Greenstein of Princeton University. Fred served as my advisor for an independent study project that I originally planned to turn into an article about Paul Wellstone's impact on politics. He encouraged me to think more ambitiously and to write a book about Wellstone's life instead. Over the course of nearly two years—long after I had completed graduate school and left Princeton—Fred guided me through the long, frustrating, and exhilarating process of writing a manuscript. He responded to my questions at all hours and provided valuable lessons in writing and research. In the hundreds of e-mails Fred sent (I saved every one), he reassured me when I had doubts, provided wise advice ("hone, sharpen, cut out all unnecessary words"), and, above all, reignited my passion for learning. At a time of personal loss, Fred became my mentor and friend, and I am immeasurably grateful.

There are many others who helped me turn this idea into a reality. The faculty and staff at the Woodrow Wilson School at Princeton University provided a community of support, and I am grateful for their friendship. Special thanks to Ambassador Robert Hutchings, Ann Corwin, Dale Sattin, John Templeton, Erica Cosgrove, Amy Craft, and Deborah Yashar. Thanks also to Professors Donald Moon, Harry Hirsch, Larry Bartels, Richard Fenno, Sy Schuster, and David Gutterman for reading manuscript drafts and providing valuable comments and suggestions.

I always wanted this to be a short, focused book rather than an exhaustive biography. Thankfully, I found Jim Reische at the University of Michigan Press, who indulged my wishes and was willing to consider the book despite its short length. Jim gave me smart advice and frequent encouragement, and I was grateful to have him in my corner.

I am blessed to be surrounded by friends and colleagues who encouraged me to see this project through. I am enormously grateful to Mark and Dave Wellstone for allowing me to write about their mom and dad and for giving me access to Paul's papers. Particular thanks to Mark, whose friendship I cherish. Thanks also to my colleagues at Wellstone Action, especially my friends and role models Jeff Blodgett and Connie Lewis.

Special thanks to Dan Luke, Laurie Stern, and Lu Lippold, the producers of "Wellstone!" a terrific documentary about Wellstone's life. They generously shared interview transcripts and other materials from their work and made my job much easier.

My parents and my sister, Annmarie Rubin, read many early versions of the book and were vocal cheerleaders. My brother, John Lofy, who on a bad day is a better writer than I will ever be, spent many hours reading manuscript drafts, giving me excellent advice, and keeping the faith. Thanks also to the entire Gutterman family for their support.

While writing this book, I spent many late nights and early mornings in front of my computer and was often distracted and frustrated by the enormity of the task at hand. Through it all, my wife, Jamie, patiently kept me on task, took me snowshoeing and fishing when I needed a break, and reminded me of why I set out to write this book in the first place.

To all I offer heartfelt thanks.

An Impolitic Politician

To take a stand, to be passionate . . . is
the politician's element, and above all
the element of the political leader.

—*Max Weber, "Politics as a Vocation"*

ON THE MORNING of October 25, 2002,
Senator Paul Wellstone, a liberal Democrat from Minnesota, was killed in a plane crash along with his wife,
daughter, and three campaign aides. Later that day, Wellstone's colleague Pete Domenici was called on to comment.
In an interview on CNN, the conservative Republican
immediately broke down in tears and was unable to continue. Several hours later, Domenici regained his composure
and agreed to another interview. He paid tribute to a senator with whom he had worked to pass legislation that would
help people suffering from mental illness, a disease that had
affected members of both men's families. The Domenici-
Wellstone mental health parity bill, which would require

insurers to treat mental illnesses the same as physical ill-nesses, had passed the Senate but was held up in the House. Addressing the dead Wellstone, Domenici promised to carry on: "You can bet, my friend, it will be started up this coming year and it will be named exclusively for you."[1]

Throughout that day, members of the political commu-nity from the full ideological spectrum paid tribute to Well-stone. "Today, the nation lost its most passionate advocate for fairness and justice for all," said Senator Ted Kennedy. "It was impossible not to like Paul Wellstone," said Senator Patrick Leahy. Paul Krugman of the *New York Times* wrote, "In an age of fake populists, Paul Wellstone was the real thing." The conservative *National Review* editorialized, "Even right-wingers must admit that he would have made a good neighbor." Conservative pundit Robert Novak admir-ingly observed that "the fighting left-wing professor from Carleton College had not altered his views, but he did soften his style." Even the Senate's most fervent conserva-tive, Jesse Helms, joined the chorus: "He was my friend and I was his."[2]

Wellstone was not always so admired.

Few new senators have landed in Washington with such an emphatic thud as Paul Wellstone. A day before being sworn into office, he pulled his green bus in front of the Dirksen Senate Office Building, a violation in the perk-con-scious capital. The following day, he held a news conference at the Vietnam Veterans Memorial, urging President George H. W. Bush not to attack Iraq. The move enraged veterans' groups and angered many Minnesotans who objected to his using the memorial to make a political state-ment. The day after that, he ignored a Senate tradition by refusing to be escorted by Minnesota's other senator to the well of the Senate chamber for his swearing-in ceremony.

He declined to be accompanied by his colleague, Republican senator Dave Durenberger, and instead asked former vice president and Minnesota senator Walter Mondale to escort him. That afternoon, Vice President Dan Quayle presided over a public swearing-in ceremony attended by reporters. As television cameras and reporters recorded the scene, Wellstone surprised Quayle by handing him an audiotape of a Minnesota town meeting in which Minnesotans express strong antiwar sentiments. In just a few days, Wellstone discovered that his abrasive style would undermine his effectiveness in Washington.

The media, Wellstone's political opponents, and even many of his allies castigated the new senator. The headlines were devastating: "A Star's Crash Landing," "Blunt Minnesota Senator Pays Price," "Wellstone Faces Fallout of Anti-War Offensive," "Under the Senate's Skin."[3] Barely into his first term, his approval rating in Minnesota was under 35 percent. Bumper stickers cropped up throughout the state: "Don't blame me: I voted for Wellstone, but I didn't think he could win." Mistrusted and disliked by many of his colleagues and alienated from Minnesotans back home, Wellstone was confronted with a crisis. "With the people of Minnesota not listening to him and the Washington bureaucrats dismissing him, Paul Wellstone is facing the possibility of becoming a six-year irrelevancy," said one political consultant.[4]

Wellstone had been warned before not to alienate his colleagues or to set overly ambitious goals. Prior to taking office, he met with Mondale, who told him that his success depended on his ability to choose his fights carefully and to produce results for his constituents. Wellstone's new colleagues Paul Simon of Illinois and Howard Metzenbaum of Ohio gave him the same advice. He ignored the advice at first, but as he settled into the Senate, it became evident that something was happening to Wellstone. The advice of Mondale and others began to sink in, and he began adjusting his style.

In a November 1991 *New York Times Magazine* article, "The Education of Paul Wellstone," correspondent Richard Berke describes a senator eleven months into his first term, with an ambitious goal: to become an outsider effective on the inside. "I want to continue to be a voice here for working with people on the outside of the process," Wellstone told Berke. At the same time, he was trying to find his own voice as a respected lawmaker. "I want," Wellstone put it simply, "to do it both ways."

He did just that, turning from a pariah into one of the capital's most admired and effective politicians. This transformation started when Wellstone recognized the importance of what he called "insider ethics": "Be on top of the legislative program, make sure your word is good and stay in close touch with colleagues, let them know what you are doing, don't blindside people." He started building personal relationships, studied the Senate rules, and learned to stay focused on a realistic number of issues. Republican senator Orrin Hatch told Berke that Wellstone was adapting well after a shaky start: "He's going to be effective around here because he's sincere and not a phony and he's willing to work." Senator Howell Heflin echoed Hatch: "He's settling back and given me the impression that he wants to be a workhorse rather than a showhorse."

While he could not yet point to a list of accomplishments, Wellstone's reputation was changing. "Nearly one year after taking Washington by storm, Wellstone is not the combatant he was," Berke concluded. "He is still feisty but he is decidedly more senatorial."[5]

Around the point when Berke's article appeared, I met Paul Wellstone. I was a sophomore at the University of Wisconsin, where I had become friends with the senator's youngest son, Mark. During Thanksgiving break, I dropped by to see Mark at his parents' modest St. Paul condominium. I remember wondering if I should be nervous in Wellstone's presence, because I wasn't. I chatted briefly with Paul and his wife, Sheila, about college, politics, and Minnesota. I was a bored nineteen-year-old art history major who was more interested in following the Grateful Dead across the country than in pursuing professional ambitions. I needed a sense of purpose and a break from school. As I left their house that day, I asked Sheila if there was any chance I could volunteer for the office. She said yes and arranged an internship for me in Wellstone's St. Paul office. I decided to take a semester off from school to see if I would like working in politics; energized by this experience, my undergraduate studies became more focused, as did my plans following graduation.

Two days after accepting my degree in 1995, I began working on Wellstone's campaign for reelection. I was his travel aide, accompanying him on all his campaign stops. We went to rallies and bean feeds, candidate forums, parades, and debates. I usually drove him by car, sometimes in his beat-up Oldsmobile. For longer trips, and when the campaign was in the final hectic weeks, we traveled on small charter planes. Usually the plane would carry four passengers plus the pilot; in the final weeks the campaign chartered larger planes, to carry more staff and the occasional reporter.

We also traveled on the vintage school bus that Wellstone had turned into a symbol of his underdog campaigns. Purchased in 1990 for three thousand dollars and painted green by a group of union autoworkers, it was an impractical means of transportation because it regularly broke down. But it was an effective political tool, attracting media attention and bolstering Wellstone's populist image. The bus had an unusable bathroom, a barely functioning heater, and a wobbly speaker's platform welded to the back. The seats had been removed and replaced with two throwaway couches and a diner-style table. Two volunteer bus drivers, retirees Paul Scott and Dick Miller, drove it across Minnesota, calculating our arrivals to allow time in the schedule for breakdowns.

Wellstone often delivered campaign speeches from the back of the bus, bringing the crowd alive with energy. Watching him speak was a physical activity. The people in the audience would rock on their heels and stand on their tiptoes as Wellstone's voice rose with excitement. At the end of his speech, he left an audience of cheering, smiling people, eager to support his campaign.

My job was perfect for getting to know Wellstone and for understanding his commitment to civic engagement. The most important thing he taught me was how to pay attention to people. I never used to strike up conversations with police officers, gas station cashiers, and waitresses. I was content to go about my business, like any normal person, without going out of my way to interact with perfect strangers. Then I started traveling with Wellstone. At each stop, he talked to everyone. At gas stations, rest stops, and cafés, he would bound in and shake hands and point at people and say, "Hi, I'm Paul. Your first name?" He loved meeting people, and I delighted in watching Wellstone's exuberant energy charge a room.

I had grown up in Minnesota, but it wasn't until I traveled with Wellstone that I realized how little I knew of the state. Now, when I'm in Duluth or Hibbing or Rochester, or when I see signs on the highway for places like Little Falls and Willmar, I remember the times I traveled to those places with him. He used to tell stories, when we were a few miles from arriving, about some person or some memory he had about the place we were going. I can picture him in those places, greeting a police officer on the street with the words "Thanks for your work, officer," or stopping to talk to the cafeteria workers at a senior center—his mother was a cafeteria worker—and thanking them for the food.

What I will remember most about Wellstone was his faith and trust in everyday people. Wellstone loved the people of Minnesota and believed in their goodness. The foundation of his political philosophy was the conviction that people want their concerns to matter to politicians. Wellstone was successful because Minnesotans, regardless of whether they always agreed with him, felt that he cared about them. They liked his honesty, appreciated his willingness to take controversial stands on issues, and saw him as one of them.

Wellstone's constituents were responding to a leadership style that he developed over the course of a career, a unique amalgam of idealism, pragmatism, and inspiration. He had high ideals and ambitious goals—equality of opportunity for all citizens, the protection of civil liberties, and a commitment to economic and social justice that placed priority on the often neglected lower- and working-class Americans— from which he refused to retreat. Yet throughout his career, he defined success as the ability to translate his ideals into results. In his two terms in the Senate, Wellstone went from outsider to respected legislator, while maintaining a group of loyal, able supporters who helped him accomplish his goals. With his powerful speaking skills and magnetic presence, he recruited a dedicated staff and a cadre of volunteers. He was a physical person who backslapped union members and offered reassuring touches to seniors and people with disabilities. It was through the laying on of hands that he won trust and moved people.

Like many others, I felt a deep compulsion to work for Wellstone. His closest friends, staff members, and advisors were people Wellstone had known for decades. Wellstone would say to his aides, "We will take this journey together," and they readily signed on. I worked for two years on his 1996 reelection campaign, and then I took my idealism abroad, serving two years as a Peace Corps volunteer in West Africa. When I returned, I went back to work for Wellstone in St. Paul. Then, after two years of working as his political organizer, I left Minnesota and started graduate school. My service for Wellstone added up to five years over the course of a decade.

I went to graduate school to study international development and made several international trips as part of my studies. I was in London's Heathrow Airport between flights on a field trip to Africa when I heard the news that Paul and Sheila, in the final days of Wellstone's campaign for a third senate term, had been killed. After a dazed moment, I canceled the second leg of my trip and booked a flight to Minnesota. For the next two weeks, I traveled with the Wellstone sons, Mark and Dave, as I had for their parents. I drove them to the funerals and joined them on campaign stops for Wellstone's replacement for his Senate campaign, Walter Mondale. The scenery and the people we saw in Duluth, on the Iron Range, and in the Twin Cities looked so familiar, and I was grateful to be back home. But, of course, the joy that I associated with those places was now replaced by overwhelming grief.

After the election, I returned to school and tried to

resume my studies in international development, but I was distracted and unsettled, thinking constantly about Wellstone and the magnitude of the loss. I requested and received permission from the school administration to devote significant time to researching Wellstone's career and potential impact on politics. Early in that process, I came upon the classic 1919 essay by the German political sociologist Max Weber, "Politics as a Vocation," a searching treatise on politics and politicians. The son of a German politician, Weber was one of the twentieth century's greatest intellectuals. He lived in the Kaiser's Germany, a political environment in which career bureaucrats like his father dominated the government. Weber viewed these politicians not as leaders but as mere administrators, engaged in favor trading and patronage. He wanted a new kind of political leader to emerge, one who had a *calling* for politics.

Weber says that such a leader is driven by high ideals but does not merely stand on the mountaintop proclaiming this vision. Those who have a true political calling also demand results. The politician who combines idealism with pragmatism is someone for whom politics is not merely a career but a vocation. Whereas a career is something a person chooses to pursue, a vocation is a summons from within, like that of a deeply religious person drawn to the priesthood.

Weber's essay was an eye-opener, and it provides this book's introductory and chapter epigraphs. The essay pointed to what is missing from most accounts of Wellstone, which picture him as an accidental politician—a college professor who in his middle years stumbled into politics. Wellstone may have been an unlikely political candidate and U.S. senator, but he spent his life engaged in what Weber called the "strong and slow boring of hard boards" that defines effective politics. For thirty years, he organized,

9

agitated, and inspired—he was never content with the status quo. Wellstone liked to say, "If we don't fight hard enough for the things we stand for, at some point we have to recognize that we don't really stand for them." He fought hard, but he knew that simply *standing* for ideals was not enough; there had to be action that led to results. He was an emotional, untiring, and optimistic man who never seemed daunted by the enormity of the challenges in front of him. He had embarked on a career in academia, but politics proved to be Wellstone's vocation.

Growing Up
an Outsider

He who lives "for" politics makes politics
his life, in an internal sense.

FOR SOMEONE WHO considered himself a
Washington outsider even after he had mastered the system,
Paul David Wellstone was born in the most unlikely of
places—the nation's capital. Born on July 21, 1944, at
George Washington Hospital in Washington, D.C., to Minnie and Leon Wellstone, he grew up in the Washington sub-
urb of Arlington, Virginia. His mother was a school cafeteria worker, and his father was a struggling writer and
government bureaucrat. Both were in their forties when
Wellstone was born.

Wellstone's father, born as Leon Wexelstein, immigrated
to the United States from the Ukraine when he was seventeen. He received a scholarship to study mathematics at the
University of Washington, leaving Russia in 1914, three
years before the Bolshevik Revolution. He would never see

his parents again. "When the Bolsheviks took over, his parents told him, 'don't come,'" Paul later recalled.[1] Wexelstein's parents later disappeared during a wave of Stalinist purges.

Upon graduation, Wexelstein worked briefly as an electrical engineer in Seattle, but he quickly realized that his true passion was for writing. He moved to New York to pursue a career as a writer, a goal that eluded him throughout his life. In New York he met and fell in love with Misha Danashevsky (known by her family as Minnie), the daughter of Jewish immigrants from Ukraine. They married and moved to Boston, where Minnie gave birth to their first son, Stephen, in 1936, and Leon landed a job writing editorials for the *Boston Evening Transcript*. After experiencing what Paul later called "virulent anti-Semitism" in Boston, Leon changed his last name to Wellstone.[2] A column he wrote about Justice Louis Brandeis of the Supreme Court attracted the attention of Harvard law professor and future justice Felix Frankfurter, who wrote Leon a laudatory note. When the *Boston Evening Transcript* shut down, Frankfurter helped him get a job as a writer in the Commerce Department in Washington, D.C. Accompanied by his wife and four-year-old Stephen, he moved to Arlington, Virginia, in September 1940.

Leon Wellstone enjoyed Washington, but despite his impressive background—he was fluent in several languages, was an accomplished mathematician, and wrote prolifically—he spent a career languishing in mid-level bureaucratic jobs. According to Eleanor Fullerton, a close family friend from Arlington, "Leon wrote many different books under different names . . . and he submitted plays in many places. He got many, many rejections."[3] Despite the repeated disappointments, he continued writing into old age, producing dozens of boxes of essays, plays, and books, nearly all of which went unpublished.

Leon spent his evenings at home, in front of a typewriter, writing journals and essays in which he expressed dismay at the state of the world, his shortcomings as a writer, his fear of death, and the issues of the day. From his writings, a picture emerges of an erudite, ponderous, and deeply troubled man. "Nobody knows me," he wrote in his journal in 1941, three years before Paul's birth. "So far I am like a guest who has not presented his visiting card, so no one knows he is around. They will know I am alive when I present my visiting card—my books."[4] But his books never found a publisher, and Leon slid into a depression that seemed to grip him for much of his life. Paul Wellstone said that his father "was someone who seemed very sad about the world."[5]

Wellstone spent several years at the Commerce Department, never giving up on his dream of becoming the next Chekhov. He left Commerce after being offered a job at the Voice of America, where he wrote anticommunist propaganda in the Russian language. Eventually, he landed at the U.S. Information Agency (USIA), which was then headed by Edward R. Murrow. He remained at the USIA until his retirement. "I remember visiting his office once," Paul told a reporter. "He was in a row of many. He didn't have any big position, and he certainly didn't have any big income."[6]

Leon Wellstone was a constant source of embarrassment for young Paul. "By age and appearance," Wellstone wrote of his father, "he just didn't fit in."[7] He was disheveled, absent-minded, and consumed with his intellectual pursuits. "Leon could never even change the fuses in his fuse box," recalled Eleanor Fullerton. "I think he was almost afraid of electricity . . . and this is from a man who had graduated in electrical engineering."[8] A social misfit with few friends and little understanding of his son's childhood interests, Leon tried to be a strong presence in young Paul's life, often with disappointing results. Wellstone recalled being embarrassed when his father would show up at his athletic events, standing alone in a trench coat and hat.

While Leon was taciturn and aloof, Minnie Wellstone was outspoken and indignant. She grew up on New York's Lower East Side, the middle daughter of a lower-class Jewish immigrant family. Her father worked as a laborer and a "junk man," going around with a horse and wagon and collecting and selling discarded items found in people's trash. Her grandfather was a garment factory worker and labor organizer who once took his granddaughter to hear the Socialist Party presidential candidate and firebrand Eugene V. Debs. Her poor upbringing and experiences with anti-Semitism led her to deeply resent the wealthy and powerful. As a youth, Paul Wellstone did not share his mother's concern for the downtrodden. In fact, Minnie's job as a cafeteria worker at Williamsburg Junior High was a source of humiliation for young Paul. "Kids would make fun of these low-income, working class women—especially their looks and the way they talked," Paul said. "I didn't want my friends to know that they were making fun of my mother."[9]

At home, Minnie told her son that there was no shame in being part of the working class. "My mother's highest tribute to a person would be, 'she's a good worker,' or 'he's a good worker,'" Paul said. "It was always important to her that people work and also that people worked under decent conditions. She was always reading the papers and interested in what was going on in the country, and she and my dad would talk about it."[10] Despite their lack of financial means, Minnie was always looking out for her friends and neighbors. "Minnie was—and I used to tell her this—the best

Christian in this neighborhood, and she was the only Jewish person in this neighborhood," said Eleanor Fullerton. "Anybody who was sick, she was right there with a pie or a cake or something. She was right there to help."[11]

Reflecting on his childhood, Wellstone said that his parents' commitment to social justice was rooted in their Jewish faith. His father had been raised an Orthodox Jew, and his mother grew up in a predominantly Jewish tenement neighborhood in New York City. Both encountered anti-Semitism as children. "[Leon's] dad was a hatter, and he had a store and over and over again [Russian] troops would come in and destroy his business," Wellstone said. Minnie Wellstone, according to her friend Eleanor Fullerton, was particularly sensitive about religious discrimination. "She used to tell me, 'You don't know. You don't remember. I remember seeing signs in banks that said NO JEWS OR CATHOLICS NEED APPLY HERE,'" Fullerton recalled. "She said prejudice was so bad."[12]

Despite strongly identifying themselves as Jews, the Wellstones did not practice their religion as adults. Paul did not have a bar mitzvah or formal religious training and once had to insist that his parents take him to synagogue, a visit that turned out to be disastrous. "Unfortunately that day the rabbi was raising money, and they were asking people to subscribe," Eleanor Fullerton said. "And that made a very bad impression on Minnie and Leon and Paul."[13] Nevertheless, the Wellstone home was steeped in Jewish tradition. Referring to the great Jewish theologians, Wellstone said, "I was raised on Abraham Heschel and Buber."[14] His father spoke fluent Yiddish and Hebrew and frequently spoke both languages around the house (he also spoke German, French, Russian, Spanish, and some Balkan languages). Wellstone's parents taught their son that his faith was necessarily connected to a struggle for justice. "I think the prophetic tradition of our faith is that to love God is to love justice," he told a Jewish newspaper.[15]

A Family Transformed

When Paul was eleven years old, his family experienced a trauma from which Leon and Minnie would never fully recover. Stephen Wellstone was starting his freshman year at Antioch College when he suffered a complete mental breakdown. A psychiatrist told the Wellstones that the only chance for restoring Stephen's health was to put him in a top hospital, so they decided to mortgage their house and check Stephen into the Phipps Psychiatric Clinic at Johns Hopkins University. Stephen's condition worsened, and after a year the Wellstones could no longer afford to pay the hospital bills. He was transferred to the less expensive Virginia State Mental Institution, where he languished for another year. Wellstone's parents spent the rest of their lives repaying the bills from his brother's two-year hospitalization.

Stephen's breakdown and subsequent hospitalization was, as Wellstone described it years later, "a radicalizing experience."[16] He witnessed the stigmatization of mental illness and the devastating impact of his brother's breakdown on his family. Wellstone visited his brother throughout his hospitalization and would later describe the horrific conditions: "decrepit buildings, patients in institutional uniforms sitting on benches or wandering aimlessly."[17] Minnie and Leon were overwhelmed. "Minnie had the saddest big brown eyes," Eleanor Fullerton said. "You'd look at them and they always had tears that you could almost see. And Leon always felt guilty that he hadn't paid enough attention to Stephen when he was a child."[18] The experience was "the worst time in my life," Wellstone once told a reporter. "It was just an awful several years."[19]

Stephen's breakdown came at a particularly formative time in Paul's life. He was just entering adolescence and had demonstrated tremendous potential as a student and a leader. In his sixth grade report card, his teacher wrote, "Paul has shown fine qualities of leadership. When he leads the class discussions he is at ease, talks well and participates freely." By nearly all measures, he was a model student, excelling at reading, spelling, math, and social studies. He had a particular talent for athletics. "Paul enjoys and eagerly takes part in all our creative and recreational activities," his teacher reported. "He possesses a keen sense of fair play and good sportsmanship."[20]

But the following year, Paul's grades began to drop, and he fell in with a group of troublemakers. He became angry and resentful that his brother's illness had consumed his parents' attention. With Leon and Minnie gone most weekends to visit Stephen, Paul began a precipitous fall into juvenile delinquency. A head shorter than the other kids and embarrassed by his short stature, he took out his frustrations by rebelling. "I was a short kid with a chip on my shoulder," he said.[21] He sought to prove his physical strength by picking fights with the kids who made fun of him. "I was a mixed-up kid—stealing cars, getting into trouble—one step, really, from reform school," he was to write.[22] From the age of eleven to fourteen, Wellstone was a young man whose life had become unhinged.

A New Passion

In the fall of 1959, Wellstone discovered the sport of wrestling. It was a perfect outlet for the tough fifteen-year-old, allowing him to channel his aggression and turn what had been a source of humiliation—his height—into a great asset. Short and muscular, he overpowered his opponents with his strength and demonstrated the fierce competitiveness that would become his trademark. He was a smart wrestler, quick to capitalize on an opponent's weakness and careful not to make himself vulnerable. He reveled in the grittiness of the sport and its lack of pretension and felt at home in the world of wrestling.

Wrestling had a profound and enduring impact on Wellstone's life. Bill Lamb, a wrestling coach and friend of Wellstone's, describes it as one of the most physically, emotionally, and mentally challenging sports. "It's just you and the other person," he said. "It's man on man, and it affects your masculinity, it affects your pride. It affects everything about you." Wrestling certainly affected everything about Wellstone. Disciplined by his new passion, he became a multisport athlete, excelling in both wrestling and long-distance running. Both sports gave Wellstone an opportunity to prove himself as an individual. "I think one of the things that attracted him [to wrestling and running] was that he got the credit, and if he didn't do well he had himself to blame," Lamb continued. "But he could deal with that because he had a chance to prove who he really was, and Paul always wanted those kinds of challenges."[23] Wellstone quickly became Yorktown High School's best wrestler, making it to the Virginia state tournament three consecutive years.

It was during his years as a wrestler that Wellstone began demonstrating a trait that would reappear throughout his life: an ability to come from behind and win. He enjoyed being the underdog and studied his opponents' strengths as carefully as their weaknesses. He would use their strength to his advantage, by redirecting their force in a way that left them vulnerable to his quickness. This ability to battle back from adversity was not limited to the wrestling mat. With new confidence, he quickly turned his life around. His grades improved dramatically, and he became a model student. "Paul has consistently increased his ability. . . . may this trend continue!" reported one of his high school teachers.[24] In addition to getting better grades, he avoided some of the vices in which some of his friends had indulged—he had one drunken experience in high school, after which he forswore alcohol, and he never once smoked marijuana.

It was during this period that Wellstone and his father grew closer, as Paul began to appreciate his father's intellect and Leon became more involved in Paul's activities. On weeknights, the two of them sat at the kitchen table and talked. With his brother incapacitated, Paul was now assuming the role of eldest son. Perhaps compensating for his previous aloofness, Leon showered attention on his son and became increasingly involved in his life. He was a frequent presence at Paul's wrestling matches, although he eventually forced himself to stay home because he could not handle the pressure. "These matches take too much out of me, even to watch," Leon wrote in an essay about Paul's final high school match. "People who have sat next to me on the benches say that I keep pushing and elbowing as if I were wrestling myself." It was probably better that Leon wasn't there: Paul lost his final match, 1–0, and missed his last chance to win the state championship. The loss was devastating, but Paul did not go through it alone. The title of Leon's essay was "We Suffer a Blow."[25]

During this period, Wellstone began turning to his father for lessons in life. "We had hot tea and sponge cake," Wellstone wrote in his book *The Conscience of a Liberal,* "and I listened to him talk about the world—all about books, ideas, writing, knowledge and education."[26] Leon taught Paul how to present an argument and to defend his ideas and told his son to take advantage of his freedom of expression. "I grew up having it drummed into me that one of the things that was great about this country was the freedom and democracy," Wellstone said. It was during this period that he realized he had the makings of a scholar and educator. "Ideas were very important to my father, so it's not surprising that I became a teacher."[27]

Sheila

In addition to maturing as a young man, Wellstone fell in love. Sheila Ison was the daughter of Southern Baptists and granddaughter of coal miners. Raised in Kentucky, she grew up in a middle-class home with two siblings; she was especially close to her homemaker mother. When Sheila was a junior in high school, the Ison family relocated to Washington, D.C., a move that left her feeling isolated and far from her Southern roots. When she was sixteen, she met Paul Wellstone at a beach in Ocean City, Maryland. Despite their different backgrounds—the Jewish son of Russian immigrants and the Christian daughter of southerners—they were immediately infatuated with one another. Paul impressed Sheila with his chiseled frame and confident demeanor—she would say later that he reminded her of James Dean. Sheila charmed him with her freckles, petite good looks, and soft voice infused with a Kentucky accent. "I would say it was love at first sight," Wellstone said. "I was always pretty shy with girls, but from the time I first met Sheila there was just something there."[28]

Paul and Sheila dated during their final year of high

school but went on to attend different colleges. He was accepted to the University of North Carolina on an academic scholarship, where he joined the wrestling team. Sheila decided to return to the South, enrolling at the University of Kentucky. By the middle of their first year of college, they could no longer stand living apart. Over winter break, Paul announced to his parents that he planned on marrying Sheila and bringing her to North Carolina. "One year, and that was it," Paul said. "I just told my mother and father that this can't go on. I just miss her. I can't do it this way. And they never opposed that."[29]

Leon remembered it somewhat differently. In an essay entitled "I Get a New Title," he wrote about his initial reservations about Paul's decision to get married. "Upon graduation [Paul and Sheila] went to different colleges," Leon wrote, "and we figured this might cool the youngsters off. It cooled off nothing, though the winter was severe." Leon remembers Paul taking him aside during a visit home and saying, "Look, Dad. We'll get along as to money, and we're very much in love. We live in an anxious world. Why wait?"[30] At first, Minnie and Leon would have none of it. "They were just overwhelmed," recalled Eleanor Fullerton. "They were so very upset. Sheila was a Christian, and they were to be married in a Christian church!"[31] Sheila's parents were also members of a local country club that had no Jewish members, a fact that particularly angered Minnie. But the Wellstones relented, knowing that Paul was certain about the decision. Leon said that after getting used to the idea he was "delighted" at what turned out to be a "positive and epochal" moment in his life. Besides, he wrote, "It was an unstoppable situation anyway."[32] Eight months later, shortly after Paul and Sheila had turned nineteen, they married.

In the fall of 1963, the Wellstones settled into a thirty-nine-year marriage. In North Carolina, Sheila got a job as a library assistant at the university, while Paul resumed what had become a rigorous academic and wrestling schedule. The Wellstones' domestic life was decidedly traditional. Although Sheila supported them financially, she assumed the role of supportive wife. "Sheila was humble and graceful and she saw her role as the person that supported Paul," said Dianne Stimson, whose husband, Jim, was a classmate of Paul's. "She was ferocious about a family and was insecure because she didn't have a college education. It wasn't that she wasn't deep and intelligent and complex . . . she just saw her role more behind the scenes."[33] It was a role that she was to play for another two decades, as a wife and mother of three. "One of the great ironies of Paul Wellstone is that he was a radical that led one of the most conservative sorts of lives," said Sam Kaplan, who was, along with his wife, Sylvia, a longtime political supporter and friend of the Wellstones.[34] Yet Sheila was hardly a submissive housewife. "Paul deferred to her even in the earliest days of their marriage," Dianne Stimson said. "I don't know of a couple that was more perfect than the two of them."[35]

The early years of their marriage were chaotic. For financial reasons, Paul had decided to finish college in three years and took more than a full load of classes. He worked two jobs, as a grocery store clerk and as the director of intramural sports at the university. His primary focus, however, was wrestling. "For me, it was all about athletics," Wellstone recalled. "Wrestling was my number one priority."[36] His college wrestling career was brief but spectacular. He went undefeated in his first season but lost in the Atlantic Coast Conference (ACC) tournament. In his second year, he again went undefeated, but this time he captured the championship that had eluded him in high school. In the championship match at the ACC tournament, Wellstone staged a stirring comeback victory in the final seconds. "Paul was behind and everything was looking bad," recalled his wrestling friend Bill Lamb. "But he didn't give up. He reached down one more time and did a fireman's carry, took the guy down to his back, and won the match."[37]

After his championship victory, Wellstone decided to end his wrestling career on top. With the pressure of school mounting, he realized that he had nothing more to prove as a wrestler and that his studies and family took priority. In fact, the Wellstone family was about to get bigger. Sheila became pregnant with their first child shortly after the end of wrestling season. The following year, she gave birth to Paul David Wellstone, who would go by the name David. Paul and Sheila were thrilled, and Paul's parents rejoiced at the addition to the family. "That they named him David was so pleasant to Minnie and Leon," Eleanor Fullerton remembered. "It was a name from the Old Testament, and Leon really believed in the Old Testament."[38]

In May 1965, two months after David's birth, Wellstone graduated from UNC after only three years. By age twenty, the near delinquent teenager had become a champion wrestler, husband, father, and college graduate.

The Making of a Political Activist

Wellstone had also become a serious student and budding political activist. When he arrived at UNC in the fall of 1962, he had little idea of what subjects interested him; he knew only that he wanted to wrestle and be with Sheila. But the civil rights movement quickly convinced Wellstone to pursue political science as a major and piqued his interest in political activism. At first, he and Sheila, consumed by their busy lives, watched as the civil rights movement exploded around them. "We saw it and we saw it, and we walked by and we walked by, because I didn't have the time," Wellstone said later. But after witnessing a Ku Klux Klan march in downtown Chapel Hill, the two saw no choice but to take action. "The KKK marched on town and there was a group of integrated white people and black people who were in the front of the post office and they were there in protest of segregation," he recalled. "They were beaten up and kicked, and we saw it. That moved me miles that night, because I just felt that we could no longer ignore what was going on."[39] Wellstone grew increasingly indignant at the treatment of blacks and scornful of the conservative establishment that supported segregation and racial prejudice. He reserved particular disdain for a conservative North Carolina radio personality named Jesse Helms, who railed against the civil rights movement in his daily commentaries on the Tobacco Radio Network.

Although Wellstone did not become a prominent civil rights activist in Chapel Hill, he nonetheless began participating in protests. He also stayed on an academic fast track after completing his undergraduate degree and decided to pursue a doctorate in political science, hoping to remain at UNC. Yet getting accepted to the UNC program would prove difficult. Despite a good academic record, Wellstone had struggled with test taking (the problem would later be diagnosed as a minor learning disability), and he received dismally low scores on the Graduate Record Examination. The university rejected his application on the grounds that he had not distinguished himself as a scholar and that he did not seem to have the ambition to become a professor.

Wellstone was enraged by the rejection. He filed a formal

protest with the admissions office, arguing that he had performed well in graduate-level courses and pointing to glowing recommendations from his professors. Wellstone had certainly taken a lesson from his initial experiences with direct action protests. He staged a sit-in at the dean's office and said he would not leave until the school reconsidered its position. Framing the issue as a clear case of injustice, he enlisted his professors to come to his defense. The strategy worked: after several days of the sit-in, the school capitulated and accepted his application. It was Wellstone's first success in protest politics.

As it turned out, the admission's office at North Carolina was right about Wellstone's lack of clarity about his career. Once admitted to the doctoral program, he seemed uncertain about why he was there. "My best memory of Paul is that he didn't really know why he was in graduate school," said his graduate school classmate and longtime friend Jim Stimson. "He wasn't comfortable with where he was going or what he was going to do."[40] Initially, he decided to specialize in Latin America because he particularly enjoyed a course in that area, but he quickly realized that he had little interest in being a professor of Latin American politics. As he continued his political activism, Wellstone settled on American politics as his specialization, with a particular focus on race and poverty.

It was during the writing of his dissertation that Wellstone came into his own as a political organizer. The dissertation, entitled "Black Militants in the Ghetto: Why They Believe in Violence," is an eighty-four-page description of the attitudes of ghetto residents in Durham, North Carolina. In 1966, violent protests against racial injustice had fractured the Durham community, and Wellstone went to investigate. He spent months interviewing poor African

Americans about their views of the police and local community leaders and found deep mistrust of government leaders, the overwhelming majority of whom were white. He developed friendships with many of the residents, despite their initial reluctance to speak openly with a white, Jewish graduate student from Washington, D.C. The experience had a deep impact on Wellstone's life. "When he met these poor people in Durham, who were really a very different part of his life because he was raised in a suburban environment, it changed his life," said Jim Stimson. "He reached into their lives and empathized with the way they lived, and he was a different person when he finished doing it."[41]

In his dissertation, Wellstone argued that ghetto residents were inclined to resort to violence and militancy because of an unwillingness of government officials to address their concerns. He rejected an argument that said the problem of militancy and rioting is simply a manifestation of psychological problems among young blacks. According to that theory, weak family structures cause young blacks to become disoriented and angry, leading them to violence and militancy. Wellstone argued that politics, not psychology, was the source of discontent among blacks in the ghetto. He asked, "Could it not be that a key variable explaining violence in the ghetto is the firm belief by ghetto residents that governmental leaders will not respond to their needs and interests?" According to his research, ghetto residents were more likely to resort to violence if they had had a "bitter personal experience with a white city official."[42]

The dissertation was a solid, if unremarkable, academic work. Heavily reliant on interviews, it was typical of Wellstone's later writings—qualitative and emotionally engaged rather than quantitative and analytically detached. "He was really torn because he was trying to be a good academic but his heart wasn't really into writing a conventional dissertation in which he used statistical methods that he didn't really believe in," Jim Stimson said.[43] The dissertation is significant not for its contribution to academic literature on the subject but because it demonstrates Wellstone's commitment to finding *political* solutions to the problems facing urban blacks. Clearly sympathetic to the subjects of his research, many of whom believed that violence was the only redress to their problems, Wellstone looked for a solution within the system. He devoted an entire chapter of the dissertation to the need for government leaders to "give ghetto residents hope that their lives will be significantly improved." Moreover, he called on political scientists to play a more active role in the policy-making process: "Social scientists must do more policy-oriented research. We live in a real world with real problems, and if we are to have any impact at all we must make our research priorities relevant. We are all quick to criticize government programs or the lack of government programs, but we do not really utilize our training and skills toward making policy recommendations."[44] He seemed poised to begin an academic career that would focus on finding practical solutions to policy problems.

Yet Wellstone was hardly pursuing a conventional path on the road to becoming a professor. He was teaching courses to undergraduates and frequently involved them in protests. "Sometimes I would take the class out to the demonstrations, which greatly added to the number of protesters," he said. In addition, Wellstone became increasingly involved in local organizing drives, including a volatile strike involving the university's cafeteria workers. Since childhood, Wellstone had witnessed the stigmatization facing his mother and other cafeteria workers, and when the workers at Lenoir Hall, UNC's main dining hall, went on strike after a wage dispute, he had an opportunity to stand up for their rights. At first, he tried to organize a boycott of the hall. When that effort failed, he tried a Saul Alinsky tactic. "There was a rule that said you had to leave the cafeteria," Wellstone later recalled. "So we would take our sweet time going through the line, sit at the tables, and just block the place up."[45]

By the time Wellstone received his Ph.D. in the spring of 1969, he had become an accomplished activist and organizer. Organizing provided him an outlet for his growing indignation at racial discrimination and economic injustice and a clear professional focus. With a newfound sense of purpose, he looked for jobs that would give him the opportunity to both teach and organize, and he gave little thought to producing large volumes of academic scholarship. During the job search, he received an offer to join the Political Science Department of a highly selective liberal arts college— Carleton College in Northfield, Minnesota. At first, he was reluctant to accept the offer. "I would have preferred staying in the south and Sheila would have too, because she's from Kentucky," Wellstone recalled. "But I think my activism in the civil rights movement hurt me at southern universities. I applied to a lot of them but I just couldn't get to first base. I came out here to interview at Carleton, and it was just one of those Minnesota days where it was 20 degrees, the sky was blue and it had just snowed, and I just loved it." At the age of twenty-four, Wellstone accepted the job. Sheila was hesitant, but Minnie and Leon approved. "When my mother heard I was going to Carleton, she said, 'That's great! Minnesota is a great state, because you don't have to be rich to take a vacation there,'" Paul said.[46]

Organizing Instead of Publishing

In the fall of 1969, Wellstone arrived in Minnesota and entered a political environment notably different from the conservatism of North Carolina. These were the glory days of Minnesota liberalism. The Democratic-Farmer-Labor Party (DFL), the product of a 1943 merger between Minnesota Democrats and the influential Farmer-Labor movement, held a vice grip on power in the state. Hubert Humphrey was returning to the U.S. Senate, where he had served since 1949, after four years as vice president under Lyndon Johnson. Eugene McCarthy was completing his second and final term in the Senate, and Walter Mondale was finishing his first term as senator.

It wasn't just Minnesota that had such a long and rich tradition of progressive populism. It was the Midwest as a whole, and Wellstone would fit into that tradition, which dated as far back as the 1800s, with such leaders as the great orator William Jennings Bryan from Nebraska. In the 1920s, populists like Robert ("Fighting Bob") Lafollette of Wisconsin and Floyd B. Olson of Minnesota ("very possibly the most radical figure ever to govern an American state"[47]) gained national prominence for their staunchly independent views, support for farmers, and relentless pursuit of progressive reform. The populists had reputations as hell-raisers ("Someone once said the populists were the sons of wild jackasses," Walter Mondale said.[48]) and were widely admired, even by their critics, for their courage to stand up for their beliefs. As one foe of Lafollette put it after seeing him deliver an emotional speech, "I hate the son of a bitch. But my God, what guts he's got."[49]

Wellstone was strongly drawn to this tradition and studied the history of the Midwest progressive populists. "This whole progressive tradition, good government tradition— that people wanted an honest politics, that people would not stand for politics that was dominated by money or dishonesty, was something that really attracted me to Minnesota," Wellstone said.[50] At Carleton College, he immersed himself in campus activism—organizing protests, criticizing the school's administration for its ties to corporate interests, and speaking out on every issue, minor and major, affecting the community. "It was clear," said Sy Schuster, one of Wellstone's Carleton friends and colleagues, "that he was less concerned about academic political science than about political science directly servicing people's needs." Wellstone frequently included community service and organizing projects as part of his classroom curriculum. "In my freshman year, Wellstone assigned us to research the welfare system in rural Rice County, Minnesota," said one of his former students, Jonathan Lange. "He took us to organizational meetings of welfare mothers, fighting to replace a food commodity program with food stamps."[51]

As a teacher, Wellstone is remembered for his passion and uncommon ability to relate to his students. When he arrived at Carleton at the age of twenty-five, his students were not much younger than he was, and they viewed Wellstone, who looked, acted, and talked like them, as a contemporary. One of his students recollected being in Wellstone's first class as a professor his freshman year:

> Like me, he wore t-shirts and jeans to class and seemed to pay scant attention to the reading list he'd assigned, except that he had an amazing command of facts that he used to support his lectures, which actually were more like speeches.

His brilliance was manifest. He was a first year teacher, so he couldn't have memorized his lectures, but he spoke without notes for an hour. He wasn't constrained by a podium, but he was predictable. Every lecture he'd start with his fingers jammed into his jeans with the thumbs hooked over the edge of the pocket, as if he were trying to restrain himself from what he must have known was coming—the inevitable rising volume, quickening cadence, and karate chopping of knowledge into our small freshman brains.[52]

Despite his strongly held views, Wellstone was also known for welcoming debate in his classes. As another student recalled, "Whether students were liberal or conservative didn't matter. He pushed us to think about what we could do to make change in the world."[53]

As a scholar, Wellstone pursued an unconventional path. He ignored conventional "publish or perish" wisdom, which says that an untenured professor without a substantial body of published scholarly work has little hope of receiving tenure. During his first two years at Carleton, he wrote only one article for a scholarly journal. Instead of producing scholarship, he concentrated on organizing. "I was determined not to be an outside observer but to use my skills as a political scientist to empower people and to step forward with people in justice struggles," he said later.[54]

Wellstone Discovers Alinsky

The greatest influence on Wellstone's thinking came not from academia but from the legendary Chicago writer and organizer Saul Alinsky. Alinsky gained prominence in the 1940s with his groundbreaking organizing work that brought together previously hostile ethnic groups in

Chicago's stockyards to form a potent social justice movement. In Alinsky's view, the goal of community organizing was to contest for power by giving people a sense of participation and belonging and by delivering results. He established coalitions that served not only as pressure groups but also as service providers that established credit unions and provided social services. The key to successfully leading economic justice campaigns was to instill a sense of possibility through pragmatism.

Alinsky's 1971 book, *Rules for Radicals*, is a blueprint for mobilizing the disenfranchised. The book sets forth a series of rules that "make the difference between being a realistic radical and being a rhetorical one." Most of the rules focus on the importance of using conflict as leverage in political struggles: "Ridicule is man's most potent weapon," "Keep the pressure on," and "Pick the target, freeze it, personalize it, and polarize it." But in other parts of the book, Alinsky concentrates on practical lessons, such as the necessity of having a sense of humor. "The organizer, searching with a free and open mind void of certainty, hating dogma, finds laughter not just a way to maintain his sanity but also a key to understanding life," he writes. "Humor is essential to a successful tactician."[55]

Wellstone learned Alinsky's lessons well. In his organizing work, he was confrontational and irreverent and embraced conflict as the central ingredient to forcing social change. But he took Alinsky's advice about maintaining a sense of humor. He is remembered as self-deprecating and jovial, with a unique talent for charming even his most vocal critics. Alinsky's writings informed Wellstone's career as both a community organizer and later a politician. He made *Rules for Radicals* required reading for his classes and even brought Alinsky to the Carleton campus to address one of his classes. He enthusiastically embraced Alinsky's emphasis on conflict and encouraged his students and fellow organizers to engage in acts of civil disobedience if necessary. "I am an old Alinsky organizer," he once said. "I believe every community has a hierarchy of power. Your job is to shake it up."[56]

Mobilizing the Rural Poor

It was in his own community that Wellstone immediately set out to shake up the hierarchy of power. With the lessons from *Rules for Radicals* freshly in mind, Wellstone began to organize poor residents of the county in which he lived. Rice County is located about forty-five miles south of the Twin Cities and at the time was home to forty-five thousand residents and only two cities of appreciable size—Northfield (ten thousand residents) and Faribault (fifteen thousand residents). Most of the residents of Rice County live in rural areas, and most of those people are poor. What Wellstone found was a type of poverty that he believed had been ignored. "The rural poor are not heirs of a tradition of political activism and attempted organization, as are many urban communities. . . . Low income residents are isolated from one another and from more affluent sectors of the community. . . . Sanctions against rural dissidents can be effectively enforced."[57]

It took Wellstone little time to start mobilizing the rural poor. In 1970, just months after arriving at Carleton, he was appointed to the board of directors of a state agency called the Rice-Goodhue-Wabasha Citizens Action Council (CAC), which had been established in 1967 with the purpose of "serving the poor."[58] He was dismayed by what he found. Instead of incorporating the voices of the poor people—mostly welfare mothers—the agency was controlled by local civic leaders, who Wellstone believed had little interest in giving poor people a participatory role in the organization. He decided to start organizing on his own. He taught an evening class for Head Start mothers and staff, using *Rules for Radicals* as a textbook. Over the course of a year, a growing number of the Head Start mothers began demanding a greater role in the CAC's formulation and implementation of antipoverty measures. They were repeatedly ignored and marginalized by the agency's leadership.

In June 1972, Wellstone and four others—two Carleton students, a mother of two on welfare, and the mother of a Head Start child—received a two-thousand-dollar grant from the United Church of Christ and formed the Organization for a Better Rice County (OBRC). One of the organizers called it "a two-fisted group that grapples with people's problems and gets things done."[59] The OBRC gained statewide recognition for its unorthodox tactics and willingness to confront existing power structures. The organization quickly made an impact. In little over a year, the organization had, among other things, filed a formal complaint against the CAC, taken a township to court over its refusal to turn over relief records, forced a school board to replace special lunch tickets for low-income students (which unnecessarily identified them to other students) with tickets that all students used, and convinced the county board to fund a day-care center with a sliding fee scale so that low-income mothers could participate.[60]

Perhaps the greatest impact Wellstone had, however, was on the self-esteem of the women involved in the OBRC. Patty Fritz, one of the founding members of the OBRC, was a low-income Rice County resident who had never imagined herself a political activist until she met Wellstone. "He gave me hope in myself," Fritz said. "He gave us tools to use." And then, Fritz said, Wellstone got out of the way and let the OBRC members organize themselves. "He wasn't really our leader," she said. "There was a real human being there, who really cared about what he was talking about. He was passionate all the time about the issues that concerned him, and those were my issues, too. I could have said the same thing, he just said it better, that's all."[61] After OBRC disbanded, Fritz played an instrumental role in unionizing the nursing home where she had worked for twenty-seven years and would later become a candidate for state legislature.[62]

Wellstone's work with the OBRC was consistent with the central theme of his dissertation research—power. Poverty, whether it is found in rural Minnesota or urban North Carolina, was primarily a political issue, not a result of psychology or pathology. For Wellstone, poverty could be understood when viewed in the context of a series of questions: Who sacrifices? Who decides? Who benefits? The answers were clear to him—the people who sacrifice in society do not have a voice. This was a theme to which Wellstone would return for much of his career. "Some people are very generous with other people's suffering," he often said.

By the end of his third year in Minnesota, Wellstone could point to an impressive list of accomplishments as an organizer. He helped raise awareness of rural poverty in Rice County, led protests against local government leaders, and trained an impressive number of students in the essentials of organizing. Above all, he enabled a cadre of poor and disenfranchised individuals to become their own leaders. "Paul wasn't the kind of organizer who sees people as objects to be organized," said former student Kari Moe, who would later serve as his chief of staff. "He really made personal relationships with the folks that he sat down and had coffee with, and talked with them. He grew to love them and they grew to love him."[63] Yet for all his successes as an organizer, Wellstone was putting his career at risk, because Carleton hired him to teach and to be a scholar, not to organize.

A Career in Peril

Wellstone's work gained the attention of Carleton's administrators, but not in the way he would have liked. They strongly disapproved of his unconventional approach to his work. In a footnote to his first book, *How the Rural Poor Got Power,* a narrative of his organizing efforts with OBRC, Wellstone wrote, "The research was attacked by various professors at Carleton on the grounds that there were no firm policy recommendations that the county commissioners and other local officials could find useful. The president of Carleton once opened a conversation with me this way: 'If I were a county commissioner I would certainly want some recommendations to go on.' The point of course was that the studies *were not for* the county commissioners."[64]

But in his dissertation, Wellstone had argued for precisely the type of scholarship that he was now criticizing. Five years after writing that political scientists should provide policymakers with concrete research, he was refusing to provide any policy recommendations with his academic research. Carleton and Minnesota seemed to radicalize Wellstone, and he was apparently carried away by the excitement of doing rather than studying. He reveled in the role of campus radical and delighted in angering the Carleton administration.

Carleton's political science scholars were unimpressed.

Without informing Wellstone, the department chair initiated an evaluation of his work in November 1973. Three months later, he came forth with a decision to dismiss Wellstone from the department. Accordingly, the dean sent Wellstone a terminal one-year contract.

The Carleton student body, led by a group of seniors, rallied to Wellstone's support. Within weeks of the announcement that his contract would not be renewed, a group of students formed the Committee to Reinstate Paul Wellstone, which led protests on Wellstone's behalf, gathered 790 signatures (out of a student body of 1,600) demanding the decision be reversed, and led a student boycott of courses in the political science department. The student newspaper made the firing a prominent and persistent story.

While student outrage mounted, Wellstone consulted Sy Schuster, a senior mathematics professor who had had earlier experience with academic freedom cases. Schuster opined that much of the evaluation of Wellstone's work at Carleton that began the previous November was in violation of Carleton procedures and that the process was unfair and biased. Schuster advised that the only way for Wellstone to maintain his position at Carleton was to work through the Carleton system, to prepare an appeal to the Faculty Affairs Committee that would claim that the manner in which he had been treated, and especially the evaluation, was in violation of Carleton's regulations. Wellstone resisted this advice at first, but soon agreed to mount an appeal if Schuster would be willing to act as his counsel.

In preparing the appeal, Schuster began investigating the evaluation and its background. His investigation revealed such obvious violations of school regulations that Dean Bruce Morgan realized that it might have inflicted serious harm on the Carleton community if heard in open testimony of the already-scheduled Faculty Affairs Committee hearing. In order to head off the hearing, the dean and President Howard Swearer prevailed on the Political Science Department to "suspend" the decision on Paul Wellstone and to agree to an evaluation by two external scholars approved by the department, Wellstone, and the administration. Thus, Professor Peter Bachrach, chair of Political Science at Temple University, and Professor Ira Katznelson of Columbia University were invited to the Carleton campus to evaluate Wellstone's teaching, scholarship, and community service; they conducted interviews with students, faculty, and administrators.

Bachrach and Katznelson wrote overwhelmingly positive assessments of Wellstone's work, which resulted in Wellstone's being granted tenure. Ironically, the Political Science Chair's hopes of getting rid of Wellstone by initiating an evaluation in his fifth year led to Wellstone being granted tenure a year earlier than other faculty who proceed through the ranks according to the standard schedule specified in the school's regulations. Wellstone was the youngest faculty member in Carleton's history to receive tenure.

Acquiring a
Political Vocation

One can say that three pre-eminent
qualities are decisive for the politician:
passion, a feeling of responsibility, and a
sense of proportion.

WELLSTONE RECEIVED TENURE in 1974
and spent the following sixteen years as the most unorthodox member of Carleton College's faculty. In addition to
meeting his teaching responsibilities, he led raucous and
often illegal protests that at times violated even Saul Alinsky's work-within-the-system radical principles. He made
no secret of his resentment of many Carleton administrators
and protested the school's hiring practices and its ties to corporate interests. He stubbornly refused to submit articles to
academic journals and instead published case studies of
grassroots organizing in which he admiringly described the
use of "guerrilla warfare" tactics in protests. Although the
subject of his courses was American politics, he said he
believed that running for office was "a waste of time."

Paradoxically, it was during this period of his life that Wellstone became a political activist. He joined the local chapter of the DFL Party and quickly became a prominent and outspoken party leader. In 1982, he was nominated to be the party's candidate for state auditor. In subsequent years, he gained prominence as a talented and ambitious political activist with a capacity for compromise. And by the end of the decade, he would be a candidate for Senate.

Despite the contradictions in Wellstone's accounts, all of this unfolded in a series of steps that in retrospect seemed logical. As a young graduate student, he viewed electoral politics as a tool in winning power struggles. Once he arrived at Carleton, he witnessed the dramatic impact he could have by engaging direct grassroots organizing. He grew disenchanted with the more indirect avenue of electoral politics. But over time, Wellstone came to believe that the reason why running for office is often an ineffective way to contest for power is that the Left had failed to apply the lessons of direct action to political campaigns. It was during his immersion in protest politics—the time of his life when he was least likely to embrace electoral politics—that Wellstone developed the techniques and leadership skills that would eventually help him become a U.S. senator.

Learning to Lead

Nowhere was the emergence of Wellstone's leadership capacity more evident than in his five-year involvement in the late 1970s with a farmer-led revolt against two utility companies in rural Minnesota. Not long after receiving tenure at Carleton, he heard about a group of farmers in the west-central part of the state who were protesting a plan to install a high-voltage power line across 430 miles of farmland. The farmers, most of whom owned small, family-run farms, argued that the power companies had chosen to build the potentially unsafe line on their land because the owners of large, irrigated farms convinced the companies that the land on the smaller farms was less productive. In fact, the owners of the irrigated farms simply did not want the line to run through their land.

The small farmers were incensed. The power line would cut through the middle of their farms, making it more difficult to plant and harvest their crops and potentially putting them in danger—the high-voltage lines used technology that had not been widely utilized before, and their safety was questioned. But above all, the farmers objected to the idea of a large power company, backed by powerful agribusiness interests and state government officials, appropriating their land. "[It] seemed like they were going to take our land, that was it, and we had nothing to say about it," said one of the farmers who helped lead the protests.[1]

When surveyors began appearing on the farmers' land in 1976, a full-scale rebellion erupted. It started with farmers chasing surveying and construction crews from their land and gradually escalated to acts of civil disobedience and violence. Angry farmers used manure spreaders to block the path of the construction workers and rammed the surveying vehicles and equipment with tractors. Eventually, the governor brought in over two hundred state troopers, almost half the size of the entire force, to quell the uprising. They were met by farmers who sprayed them with ammonia and threatened them with baseball bats. The protests riveted the state and attracted national media attention.

Wellstone worked at the center of this struggle. Early on, he began participating in protests with the farmers and worked to get to know the families involved. He and a Carleton physics professor named Mike Casper, an experienced community organizer and close friend who would forge a long and close partnership with Wellstone, started traveling to the area regularly, lending advice to the protesters. So taken by the protests were Casper and Wellstone that they decided to chronicle the experience in a 1981 book, *Powerline: The First Battle of America's Energy War*. Although the book provides a detailed account of the controversy, what stands out are not the tactical lessons that the authors suggest but rather their treatment of the participants. Wellstone spent countless days with the protesters and their families, interviewing them for the book, joining them in the protests, and borrowing their living room floors for a place to sleep. He admired the protesters, and they clearly trusted him. The book devotes sections of each chapter to sympathetic profiles of the participants, and Wellstone seemed intent to let them tell their own story through his words. "What I think Paul was so good at was listening and getting you to express what you were about," recalls Patti Kakac, who was working on her parents' dairy farm when she joined the protests. "I talked about my feelings for the land, and how I felt the environment needed to be preserved, and what he did—I can't remember specifically his words—was give me assurance that I knew what I was talking about."[2]

The power line struggle marks an important period in Wellstone's development as a politician. While he had already demonstrated a gift for inspiring his students at Carleton, it was not until he arrived in the harsh environment of western Minnesota that his leadership capacity stood out. Wellstone was working in a deeply conservative area of the state, where strangers are viewed suspiciously. He was a short, Jewish college professor with an Afro haircut and no background in farming or agriculture. Yet the local farmers accepted and even embraced him. "Having people like Paul there . . . was a very empowering thing for the communities," said one of the leaders of the protest.[3] If Wellstone's participation was empowering to the protesters, it was equally beneficial to him. As one of his old friends described it, Wellstone was learning to speak to a new constituency. "Paul was always interested in speaking to people where they were," David Morris recalled. "His background was in civil rights in North Carolina, so he spoke to people of a different color, and in this case he was speaking to farmers and to rural communities. . . . this was part of his learning to listen and learning to lead."[4]

He was also learning to speak eloquently. Always articulate and personable, Wellstone was developing a persuasive speaking style that recalled the great progressive orators of the early twentieth century. Like former presidential candidate Eugene V. Debs, whom his mother went to see as a small child in New York City, Wellstone had a particular talent for using cadences to build a speech to a crescendo. He rarely spoke from prepared remarks or even used notes, preferring instead to memorize speeches or to speak off the cuff. This was a practice that he would continue for the rest of his career, with the exception of when he delivered policy speeches on the floor of the Senate. With this spontaneous delivery and impassioned style, Wellstone had an unusual ability to connect with audiences and to move them to action. "You've heard Paul speak, you know how Paul can talk," said a participant in the power line protests. "You know how he can go to the heart of a matter and help people understand not only what's wrong but what's right and where there's hope."[5] He moved audiences with a preacher-in-the-pulpit style that Minnesotans had not seen since Hubert H. Humphrey.

Flourishing

By the end of the 1970s, Wellstone was not only an accomplished organizer and speaker; he was also flourishing at Carleton. He was well liked by students and was regularly voted "Best Professor" in the school's annual student survey. He also demonstrated that, when motivated by the right subject matter, he could publish scholarly material. In early 1981, he and Casper completed *Powerline*, a 314-page narrative of the controversy. While lacking in theoretical grounding, the book is an engaging description of citizen activism and a more cogent narrative than Wellstone's previous book. Although it was not a groundbreaking study, the book was well received. "If Minnesota farmers fought the first battle in America's energy war, *Powerline* is its manifesto," wrote one reviewer.[6]

Meanwhile, Wellstone had become a prolific writer and commentator on current events in the Minnesota press. He was a frequent guest columnist for Twin Cities' newspapers and public radio, displaying a mastery of policy issues as wide-ranging as farming, nuclear freeze, and poverty. He read voraciously, collecting piles of newspaper clippings with handwritten notes in the columns. Like his father, Wellstone had an almost obsessive preoccupation with current affairs and was determined to make his opinions relevant to people in positions of power. He spoke frequently to social justice groups, human rights advocates, peace activists, and farming groups, frequently running himself into a state of exhaustion. By the end of the 1970s, he had developed a reputation as one of Minnesota's leading liberals.

At the same time, Wellstone had settled into domestic bliss in his personal life. With the birth of their youngest son, Mark, in 1972, Paul and Sheila had become the proud parents of three children. While not particularly interested in politics, David and Mark would quickly follow in their father's footsteps as wrestlers. David was sidelined by injury and was forced to quit the sport in high school, but Mark achieved a goal that had eluded his father by becoming a state champion wrestler, winning the high school championship despite having a badly torn knee ligament (he went on to wrestle at the University of Wisconsin but was forced to quit because of the knee injury). Paul and Sheila were fanatical wrestling fans—Sheila never missed a single match that her kids took part in, and Paul was known for energetically rooting for his kids. "You should see him at my wrestling matches," Mark told a reporter in 1990. "I don't ever see it, but everyone tells me it's not safe to sit within 10 feet of him."[7] Their daughter, Marcia, was an energetic and thoughtful girl who wrote adoring cards to her parents and had an especially close relationship with her father. Like her brothers, she excelled in sports and was popular in school. To her parents' great satisfaction, she would go on to pursue a career in teaching.

Despite Paul and Sheila's traditional marriage, life in the Wellstone house was hardly conventional. Paul's students were constantly calling the house or stopping by to meet with him, and he was frequently traveling to organizing meetings throughout the state. As parents, the Wellstones were not strict disciplinarians—the children were given significant freedom to pursue their interests and goals—but they trusted their kids and provided them with a strong, loving family structure. In an unpublished autobiography, Paul writes about his regret at not being enough of a presence in his children's lives when they were younger, but by all accounts he was an attentive father who loved his children ferociously. At home, he tried to instill in his children the values he spent a lifetime upholding. "He wasn't wishy-washy," David recalled. "He always stood up for things that were important. He really tried to teach us social justice, social consciousness."[8]

By the end of the 1970s, Wellstone was thriving. He had a great family and successful marriage, and he had matured not only as a professor but also as a leader. The resurrection of Wellstone's career represents a pattern that repeated itself throughout his life. He was doing well as a professor and still managed to engage in the same organizing activities that had imperiled his career. Just as he had done as a teenager, he was harnessing his anger into constructive activity; as a result, Wellstone had used his experience as a radical community organizer to publish a serious academic book. He was a man of passion who was prone both to go off the rails and to bounce back, learning from experience and moving on. But he began the 1980s by overreaching again, making an ill-advised and premature foray into elective politics.

The First Campaign

Emboldened by his experience with the power line protests, Wellstone possessed a growing self-confidence that appeared brash in light of his next decision: to seek statewide elective office. In the spring of 1982, he puzzled his family and friends by announcing his candidacy for state auditor, a position that would have put him in charge of overseeing the state of Minnesota's accounting and auditing activities. It was an office that he was singularly unqualified to hold. He had little interest in budgetary matters and a limited understanding of the job. The learning disability that had made it difficult for him to take standardized tests also affected his ability to read charts and graphs. He was unfit for the job and woefully underfunded, but Wellstone was confident that he could win the support of a majority of delegates by presenting a bold agenda that had little to do with the job of state auditor.

He was right. Throughout the spring, Wellstone traveled to DFL Party candidate forums and local nominating conventions and made personal appeals to delegates to the state convention. With a campaign budget of less than two thousand dollars, he could barely afford the cost of long-distance calls to delegates, yet he proved to be a highly effective campaigner. Wearing a borrowed tie (he owned none) and his only sport coat, he went to DFL gatherings across the state, taking his campaign to the delegates. By the time the state convention began in early June, he had become the front-runner in a three-way race that featured two candidates with years of experience in accounting and government finance.

On June 5, Wellstone addressed the twelve hundred exhausted delegates to the state DFL convention. It was the convention's last day, and delegates had just finished an arduous nomination process for the party's candidates for U.S. Senate. When Wellstone took the stage, the crowd barely noticed. "I seek your endorsement to run as the DFL candidate for state auditor," he began. "I am running because I love my country and I love my state, and I am worried about our survival—our economic survival in the face of the threat of nuclear war." For the next fifteen minutes, he ignited the crowd with a speech that addressed few issues related to the job of managing the state's budgetary affairs. Instead, he called for a nuclear freeze, antipoverty programs, environmental action, and economic justice. "As state auditor, I will speak out to provide leadership on critical national issues," he continued. "Some say that a state official has no business talking about the nuclear arms race, that it is a national issue. I say the survival of Minnesotans is a Minnesota issue!"[9] It was exactly what the delegates wanted to hear. Unconcerned about Wellstone's lack of qualifications for the job, they endorsed him by acclamation.

Wellstone went on to face incumbent Arne Carlson, a popular moderate Republican with a background in business. The campaign was over soon after it began. At a debate, Carlson attacked Wellstone for not having the analytical skills to fulfill the job of auditor. Carlson cited testimony that Wellstone had given at a utility rate hearing case three years earlier, in which Wellstone said he "couldn't read graphs and charts and figures" and that he was unable to "put together an eight-piece puzzle" for his kids.[10] Wellstone had no effective response to his own words, and the attack was widely covered in the press. He lost by ten percentage points.

Wellstone's decision to run for auditor exemplified his capacity to get carried away with his passions. It is not just that he overreached by running for statewide office as a little known political novice; he also had no credibility when it came to the substance of the job he sought. The episode suggests a lack of seriousness on Wellstone's part—could he really have believed that the people of Minnesota would want him in charge of the state's top fiscal agency? While Wellstone's campaign platform provided for an entertaining election, his clear lack of interest in the substance of the job of auditor bordered on irresponsible. He seemed to view his candidacy for auditor as simply an extension of his organizing efforts. Voters expect more from their candidates, and Wellstone learned that, if he wanted to be taken seriously as

a general election candidate, he would have to give Minnesotans a credible rationale for voting for him.

But if the campaign for auditor taught Wellstone about
the difficulty of appealing to mainstream voters, it also
taught him some valuable lessons. In a journal he kept
throughout the campaign, he wrote of his frustrations and
successes. He recognized early on that he often overreacted
to criticism. "I've got to get thick-skinned," he wrote. The
journal also shows Wellstone learning how to campaign.
"At parades, I can work the crowds, and I need to keep saying my name instead of saying 'DFL,'" he wrote. "People
want a Hubert H. Humphrey—someone who will fight."[11]
Indeed, Wellstone was demonstrating an unusual capacity
to inspire thousands of rank-and-file DFL Party activists.
That he came from relative obscurity to win the DFL
endorsement demonstrated that he had a rare talent for
moving an audience. Under the right conditions, with a
more appropriate elective office and more time to put
together a campaign, Wellstone sensed that he could use a
future DFL endorsement to propel him to the forefront of
Minnesota politics.

Gaining Credibility

After his failed bid for auditor in 1982, Wellstone remained
active in DFL politics, hoping to build a network of friends
within the party. Like other potential office seekers, he
wanted to maintain a reservoir of support for a potential run
for office by becoming a constant presence at party func-
tions and being seen as a champion of the party's interests.
He was very well known and vocal in DFL circles and
understood the importance of maintaining close personal
relationships and of building trust with the party activists.

But Wellstone took an unconventional approach to such networking. In 1984, he used the support he had garnered from the auditor's race to win appointment as a member of Minnesota's four-person delegation to the Democratic National Committee. It was a logical decision that would have been unremarkable but for the fact that he was an outspoken supporter of presidential candidate Jesse Jackson, who was running against an icon of Minnesota liberalism, Walter Mondale. Instead of working for Minnesota's favorite son, he chose to work for a candidate who stood almost no chance of getting elected and whose ties to Minnesota were weak. It was an odd way to build a network of potential supporters, but Wellstone was determined to do things his way. He understood the potential negative consequences of alienating Mondale's supporters but placed a higher value on speaking his mind and supporting the candidate of his choosing. It did not seem to concern him that his support of Jackson might undermine his future chances at running for office.

Nor did Wellstone hesitate in calling for dramatic changes in the Democratic Party. He wrote long memos to party leaders and delegates in Minnesota, describing the party as "dominated by big money and rarely challenging the prerogatives of corporate capitalism." Wellstone bemoaned the Democratic Party's obsession with fielding centrist political candidates and focusing on "the politics of strategy and tactical planning." Instead, he wrote that Democrats could only win if they presented a bold agenda that clearly differentiated their policies from those of the Republicans. "This is no time for timidity," he wrote in a typical missive to party activists. "It is time to organize and fight back. Our party has always been at its best when it has been a part of the social justice struggles of the time."[12]

Paul and his older brother, Stephen, whose mental breakdown as a young man left Wellstone's parents heartbroken and deeply in debt. Wellstone later described Stephen's illness as a "radicalizing experience."

After a precipitous fall into juvenile delinquency, Wellstone turned his life around in high school and became a top student and star athlete, excelling in both wrestling and cross-country.

Wellstone married Sheila Ison in the summer of 1963. Their thirty-nine-year marriage was an unusually close partnership, with Sheila playing a central role in all of Paul's major decisions and later becoming a national advocate for victims of domestic violence.

Wellstone went to the University of North Carolina, where he became an Atlantic Coast Conference champion wrestler. He quit wrestling after two years to focus on his studies and his family. By the age of twenty, he was a college graduate, champion wrestler, husband, and father.

Wellstone speaking at a Carleton College protest. Rather than publishing journal articles and conducting traditional academic research, he concentrated on organizing and social activism and led protests against several of Carleton's trustees. (Photo from the Carleton College archives)

In 1982, Wellstone made an unlikely run for state auditor, a position for which he later admitted he was unqualified. Instead of concentrating on the state's budgetary issues, Wellstone's campaign focused on nuclear disarmament and social justice. He lost by over ten percentage points.

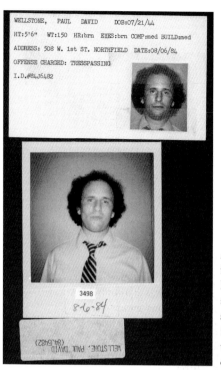

After leading a protest against farm foreclosures at a central Minnesota bank, Wellstone was arrested for trespassing along with several of his Carleton students, including one, Jeff Blodgett, who would go on to manage all of his campaigns for the Senate.

Wellstone began his quixotic bid for the Senate in 1990 by appealing to the delegates of the Minnesota Democratic-Farmer-Labor Party with a simple slogan: "This time, vote for what you believe in." (Photo used by permission of Terry Gydesen)

Exhausted at the end of nearly two years of nonstop campaigning, Wellstone was stung by Rudy Boschwitz's last-minute letter to members of Minnesota's Jewish community, which questioned Wellstone's commitment to the Jewish faith. The letter backfired and gave Wellstone a surge of momentum going into the final weekend of the campaign. (Photo used by permission of Terry Gydesen)

Wellstone's first week as a senator was disastrous. He angered veterans' groups, his new Senate colleagues, and President Bush (who was overheard calling Wellstone a "chickenshit"). When he was officially sworn into office, Wellstone gave Vice President Dan Quayle an audiotape of Minnesotans expressing opposition to the pending Gulf War. The move outraged Quayle and led several senators to question Wellstone's ability to be effective.

Over time, Wellstone began to soften his style, befriending such veteran Democratic senators as Paul Simon (left), Howard Metzenbaum, and James Exon and such Republican senators as Ted Stevens and Orrin Hatch. By the end of his first year in the Senate, he had become, in the words of one reporter, "an emerging force to be reckoned with."

After Republicans swept into control of Congress in 1994, Wellstone was a constant irritant to the new majority party. His efforts to block elements of the "Contract with America" led the Republican Party to make Wellstone their top congressional target for defeat in 1996. (Cartoon used with permission of the Minneapolis-based *Star Tribune*)

After a successful first term, Wellstone would face his old foe, Rudy Boschwitz, in his 1996 reelection campaign. Despite enjoying the overwhelming support of his liberal supporters, Wellstone ran into trouble when he announced his support of a federal ban on gay marriages known as the Defense of Marriage Act. Days after announcing his support of the ban, Wellstone went to the annual Gay Pride celebration in Minneapolis, where he was confronted by angry supporters. (Photo used by permission of Terry Gydesen)

Wellstone and the author on the green bus during the 1996 campaign. (Photo used by permission of Terry Gydesen)

Wellstone makes his way to the stage to give his victory speech on election night in 1996. His decisive victory over Boschwitz solidified his position as the state's leading Democrat and silenced critics who said that his 1990 victory was a fluke. (Photo used by permission of Terry Gydesen)

Wellstone and the man who would replace him on the 2002 ballot, former vice president Walter Mondale. Mondale, who Wellstone chose to escort him to the well of the Senate when he first took the oath of office in 1991, was a friend and mentor to Wellstone throughout his tenure in the Senate. It was Mondale who originally counseled Wellstone to settle in to the Senate slowly by observing his colleagues, learning the rules, and focusing on a few issues.

Paul and Sheila Wellstone on the back of the green bus in 2002 with a group of veterans. Wellstone would later describe his unusually close relationship with veterans' groups as one of the greatest accomplishments in his career. At far left is Marcia Wellstone, who took a leave of absence from her high school teaching job to campaign full-time with her parents.

As Wellstone was chastising the Democratic Party for failing to organize the electorate, he continued his own community organizing efforts. In the mid-1980s, he got involved in two divisive incidents that a traditional politician would have avoided: a series of farming-related protests and a violent strike by factory workers in southern Minnesota.

The farm protests began when farmers were hit by a devastating combination of plummeting land prices, higher interest rates, and reduced federal payments to agriculture. Many small farmers held heavy debt loads as a result of low interest rates in the 1970s, and they were left without the means to repay their loans. Banks foreclosed on the loans, seizing land and auctioning farm equipment. Many farmers resisted and often threatened violence against bank officials and auctioneers who entered their land.

As he had done during the power line struggle, Wellstone helped lead protests on behalf of the farmers, staging sit-ins at banks and organizing rallies at the state capitol. In 1982, he was arrested for trespassing at a bank in the central Minnesota town of Paynesville after leading a protest.

Along the way, he listened and learned. Not only did his organizing efforts help establish him as a leading liberal activist in Minnesota, but they also gave him an extraordinary opportunity to learn the intricacies of agriculture policy. For someone interested in running for office in Minnesota, where agriculture is one of the most important issues, understanding the experience of farmers and the policies affecting them is critical. Having spent so much time in rural Minnesota, Wellstone had become fluent in the language of family farmers. He knew the prices of commodities, understood the causes of the farm crisis, and could communicate the concerns and demands of the farmers who were affected by the foreclosures. His familiarity with rural Minnesota would pay a huge dividend when he needed to assemble a statewide grassroots political campaign.

But first Wellstone became a key participant in a strike at the Hormel meatpacking plant that divided the town of Austin, Minnesota, and left almost seven hundred union workers out of work. After a protracted contract dispute, members of Meatpacker Local P-9 walked off their jobs and stayed on strike for over five months before Hormel reopened the plant and threatened to hire permanent replacement workers. The union leadership stood firm in the face of the threat, but some members returned to work. Some of the strikers reacted to the defections and the hiring of scab workers by smashing windows, preventing workers from getting to work, and threatening them with violence. When Governor Rudy Perpich—the same Democrat with whom Wellstone had clashed during the power line struggle—called in the National Guard to preserve order and keep the plant operating, Wellstone pressured him to use his influence to force a settlement. At the same time, he urged the union leadership to find a face-saving way out of the controversy.

In the end, the strike failed. In addition to losing their jobs, the striking workers received little sympathy from a public that opposed their violent methods. Wellstone was depressed, feeling that he had let the workers down. But he was also praised for his role as an intermediary between the striking workers and the governor. "As in his earlier involvement in the farm protest," write the journalists Dane Smith and Dennis McGrath, "Wellstone's true role in the Hormel strike was that of a realist who worked behind the scenes to bring about a resolution."[13] Although his association with the unpopular strike would become a political liability when he ran for the Senate, the incident demon-strated Wellstone's strong pragmatic streak.

By 1988, Wellstone had cultivated a vast network of friends and political allies across Minnesota and was proficient in political organizing and advocacy. When Jesse Jackson ran again that year for president, Wellstone was a logical choice to cochair his campaign in Minnesota. Despite his reservations about Jackson's perceived insensi-tivity to Jews (Jackson had referred to New York City as "Hymietown"), Wellstone agreed to take the job, and he managed the campaign adeptly. Although Jackson lost the Minnesota caucus to Michael Dukakis, he performed remarkably well, winning 20 percent of the delegates in a field of seven candidates. Political observers were stunned by Jackson's showing and credited Wellstone with galvaniz-ing an impressive base of Jackson supporters in a nearly all-white state.

Wellstone was also cementing his reputation as one of the best orators in the DFL Party. Scott Adams, a Jackson organizer who became one of the architects of the 1990 Sen-ate campaign, said that when Wellstone spoke on Jackson's behalf at party events he energized the room. "One time in western Minnesota there were two little old ladies sitting in the back row, and Paul spoke and brought the crowd to their feet," Adams recalled. "These two ladies were not support-ing Jackson, but they were on their feet, they were clapping, and they were saying, 'I just wish he'd run for something!'"[14] After Wellstone gave another fiery speech at the 1988 state DFL convention, Adams, along with a small group of Jack-son campaign activists, began suggesting to Wellstone that he run for Senate in 1990. "We were sitting around a campfire after the first day of the convention, and we said, 'Let's get him to run for Senate, he can win,'" Adams said.

"So we decided we were going to get everyone we knew on the convention floor to address Paul as 'Senator.' So people did that, and Paul said, 'Aw, come on you guys, cut it out,' but we kept peppering him, and we planted the seeds in his head."[15]

If Wellstone's speaking ability caught the attention of delegates, DFL Party insiders were equally impressed with his willingness to work with the victorious Dukakis campaign. He was gracious in defeat. He formed an immediate alliance with Dukakis's Minnesota director, Pat Forceia, and set out to turn Jackson supporters into active Dukakis supporters and volunteers. Shortly after the February caucuses, Wellstone was named a cochair of the Dukakis campaign. Despite Dukakis's sound defeat in the general election, Wellstone had demonstrated both before and after the DFL caucuses that he had learned how to compromise and to forge political alliances.

By the end of 1988, Wellstone found himself in an unlikely position. He was still an outspoken and radical community organizer and had gained prominence for his support of a presidential candidate who was in the race to make a statement and did not have a chance for victory. Yet he was clearly moving toward becoming an effective electoral politician. He demonstrated considerable leadership potential and an ability to move people with his oratory. He was a gifted organizer, having led Jackson's symbolic campaign to a surprisingly good showing. And he showed that he was not merely interested in making a point—despite having reservations about Dukakis, Wellstone was unquestionably committed to helping him win the presidency.

Encouraged by his friends, Wellstone began exploring the possibility of running for statewide office again. "Because of what I'd seen in '88, I thought there was a lot of enthusiasm in the state for a different kind of politics," he said. "Jackson's appeal was rather astounding in Minnesota. I thought it had a lot to do with the message. I could see that a populist type of campaign could maybe catch fire."[16] But Wellstone knew that, just as important as his message, he possessed oratorical and organizing skills that would first inspire people and then turn them into an army of volunteers. Early in 1989, *Mpls.St.Paul Magazine* named him "Best Speaker of the Twin Cities," reporting that "audiences across Minnesota grow quiet when Paul Wellstone speaks."[17] Rumors began circulating that he was considering a run for Senate. In a January 1989 article in the Carleton student newspaper, Wellstone did little to dampen the speculation. "I would love doing this," he said. "It would be a truly unorthodox campaign . . . that would capture the imagination of people."[18]

Tilting a Seeming Windmill

Rudy Boschwitz was in 1988 a highly popular Republican senator with two years remaining on his second term. A self-made millionaire, Boschwitz fit in easily among Washington power brokers, but he also conveyed a down-home, plaid-shirt appeal to Minnesota voters. With approval ratings hovering above 70 percent, Boschwitz seemed virtually unbeatable. DFL Party activists were dismayed. Their 1988 nominee for Minnesota's other U.S. Senate seat, Hubert H. Humphrey III, had just lost badly to the Republican incumbent, David Durenberger. Worse, Boschwitz had been amassing a huge campaign war chest. Unlike most politicians, Boschwitz enjoyed raising money, and he had a seemingly endless supply of fund-raising sources.

Yet Boschwitz's perceived invincibility presented Wellstone with an opportunity. By his calculation, he had nothing to lose by running for Boschwitz's seat. While more established candidates, such as former vice president Walter Mondale, passed on taking on such a strong incumbent, Wellstone began planning a campaign. After a series of meetings with friends and supporters, he headed to northern Minnesota's Iron Range to seek the advice of his friends in that legendarily Democratic region of the state. In conversations with union leaders and local activists—people Wellstone had known for years from his organizing days—he heard palpable frustration about the DFL Party's inability to field inspiring candidates. The meetings confirmed his belief that the only person who could defeat Boschwitz would be someone who could galvanize a loyal, active following and, as Wellstone liked to say, "raise hell."

In the spring of 1989, Wellstone gathered a group of his advisers for a final discussion about the advantages and disadvantages of running for Senate. Some of the members of the group, including his friend from the Dukakis campaign, Pat Forceia, urged him to consider a run for chair of the state DFL Party. "Pat tried to tell Paul that if he ran for Senate and lost, his political career will be over," recalled Scott Adams. Forceia urged him to use a run for party chair as a launching pad for a later Senate race. "But Sheila said, 'I'm not losing my husband for a year and a half for him to become party chair. Paul wants to be senator, he wants to run for Senate, and that's what he should do.'"[19] That settled it. In April 1989, he announced that he would run for Senate.

Wellstone decided that his only chance for winning the party endorsement was to present himself to delegates with a simple appeal: "This time, vote for what you believe in." Like he had done as a young wrestler, Wellstone wanted to

turn his perceived weakness—in this case, his liberalism—
into his greatest strength. "We knew what we needed to do,"
said Scott Adams. "Organize the caucuses. Bring all the
Jackson people in and keep them there. Work the progressive, peace and justice, activist community. And secure the
Iron Range—the steelworkers and the unions."[20] Wellstone
threw himself into the campaign with all his energy. He
became a fixture on the Iron Range, sleeping on the couch
of his friends and supporters Gabe and Mary Ann Brisbois,
speaking at union gatherings and house parties, and standing outside plant gates to shake hands with workers. When
he was back home in Northfield, he spent every evening on
the phone, calling potential delegates to the DFL state convention, trying to convince them to support his fledgling
candidacy.

The DFL Party endorsement was critical to Wellstone's
success. Without it, a candidate can run in the party's
autumn primary but lacks the name recognition, voter lists,
and financial resources that come with the party's endorsement. To get the endorsement, a candidate needs the support of a majority of party delegates, starting at the precinct
caucuses (where party members begin the process of choosing delegates for the state convention) and ending with the
convention itself. The endorsement process played to Wellstone's strength. With a relatively small universe of caucus
attendees, he needed to speak directly to as many potential
delegates as possible.

Wellstone implemented a four-part strategy to win the
endorsement. First, he traveled throughout the state to meet
the rank-and-file delegates whose support was essential for
an endorsement. Second, he began forging a coalition of
supporters from disparate parts of the DFL's constituency—
union members, environmentalists, peace activists, and oth-

ers. Third, he organized these supporters into a network of volunteers who made phone calls and knocked on the doors of potential delegates. Fourth, he flooded the precinct caucuses with his supporters, surprising observers by securing a clear plurality of support.

For over a year, Wellstone worked the party activists at the grass roots, and his efforts paid off. In June 1990, the DFL Party held its endorsement convention, where signs of Wellstone's organizational superiority were immediately obvious. His staff, most of whom were in their early twenties, had come to the convention well prepared, and they dispatched teams of supporters—and Wellstone himself—to speak to the delegates. Wellstone's organization, combined with his electrifying speeches, overwhelmed his opponents. Despite reservations about his electability, the delegates endorsed him after a long night of balloting. Wellstone was ecstatic. "I promise you a campaign that will light a prairie fire that will sweep Rudy Boschwitz and all his money out of office," he shouted to the delegates.[21]

But first he would need to win the DFL primary in September. Wellstone's primary opponent was Jim Nichols, the state agriculture commissioner. The pro-life Nichols drew most of his support from farmers in rural Minnesota and from the state's most powerful antiabortion organizations. Nichols was well known and highly respected, and polls showed him leading Wellstone up to the day before the September primary. For his part, Wellstone had been replicating his DFL endorsement strategy, dispatching hundreds of volunteers across the state to call and knock on the doors of potential DFL voters. He focused on bringing new voters into his base; once committed, his supporters promised to go to the polls and vote. They carried through on their promise and gave Wellstone a decisive victory. Despite polls that showed Nichols in the lead, Wellstone cruised to victory with 60 percent of the vote to Nichols's 35 percent.

Wellstone had little time to celebrate. Boschwitz was awaiting Wellstone with full campaign coffers, high approval ratings, and the confidence of a two-term incumbent. Worse for DFLers, Paul Wellstone held positions far to the left of mainstream Minnesotans and had a campaign account balance of almost zero. A poll released after the September primary showed him trailing by eighteen points, an encouraging sign for Wellstone, whose own polling showed him trailing by thirty-three points a few months earlier, but a huge gap nonetheless. Boschwitz himself predicted that he would win reelection by twenty points. "Paul is certainly not as strong a candidate as might have been fielded," he told reporters.[22]

Wellstone ran against Boschwitz's wealth, portraying him as an agent of the elite. He attacked Boschwitz relentlessly, using the senator's twelve-year voting record as evidence of his neglect of working-class Minnesotans. "Boschwitz says we don't have the money to deal with education, child-care, health care, the environment," Wellstone said in his stump speeches. "He is willing to spend $500 billion to bail out the savings and loan industry, and $300 billion dollars a year for the Pentagon. I say we will have no real national security unless we invest in our people, our communities, our economy." Wellstone laced his fiery speeches with disarming humor, arguing that, unlike Boschwitz, he would be a senator for the "little fellers, not the Rockefellers." He argued, "Rudy Boschwitz is the senator from Exxon. I'll be the senator from now on."[23]

It was a tough sell. Despite his popularity among DFL Party members, Wellstone had a reputation as a rabble-rousing liberal. He had virtually no name recognition, no professional staff, and no money. His views were more liberal than those of mainstream Minnesotans, and with his disheveled appearance and frantic mannerisms, Wellstone looked decidedly unsenatorial. He proudly admitted that he had not had a professional haircut since high school (Sheila was his barber), that he owned only one suit, and that he had never worn a tuxedo in his life. In fact, Wellstone barely looked the part of a college professor, since he regularly taught classes in jeans, a T-shirt, and running shoes. Even his closest advisers were skeptical about his chances. "It was," said Jeff Blodgett, his three-time campaign manager, "a suicide mission."[24]

Wellstone had so little money that he could hardly afford to run any television advertisements, a potentially fatal weakness in light of Boschwitz's ability to purchase a seemingly endless number of ad spots. Desperate to break through to a wide audience, Wellstone relied on a risky television advertising strategy that injected into the campaign what would be one of his greatest weapons: humor. His advertising consultant, a former Carleton student named Bill Hillsman, produced an ad that begins with Wellstone saying, "I'm Paul Wellstone and I'm running for United States Senate. Unlike my opponent, I don't have $6 million, so I'm going to have to talk fast." Wellstone then races frantically past the screen, past hospitals and farm fields and senior citizen centers, promising to lead the fight for national health care, to protect the environment, and to advocate for senior citizens. Another ad, which the campaign could afford to run only once, showed Wellstone trying to track down Rudy Boschwitz for a debate. Based on Michael Moore's documentary "Roger and Me," the two-minute ad had Wellstone searching for Boschwitz at his campaign office and Senate office. It ends with Wellstone on the telephone, calling information to locate Boschwitz's home telephone number to no avail.

The commercials themselves became a campaign story and provided Wellstone with much-needed attention. Television stations ran news stories on the ads, replaying them on the nightly news. Within days of their release, the entire state seemed to be talking about Wellstone's campaign commercials. On his campaign stops, Wellstone was overwhelmed by people asking him, "Did you find Rudy yet?" Suddenly, people were paying attention to this unknown and quirky candidate for U.S. Senate.

Boschwitz played into Wellstone's strategy perfectly. Confident of victory, he ignored Wellstone for months, refusing to give the unknown liberal a platform. The plan backfired. By the middle of October, Wellstone started showing signs of movement and the Boschwitz campaign was getting nervous. In a sign of desperation, Boschwitz struck back by attacking Wellstone as an "Abbie Hoffman-type character," a "leftist hustler," and a "self-promoting little fake."[25] The attack served only to solidify Boschwitz's image as humorless and defensive, and Wellstone's camp seized on the misstep, suggesting that Boschwitz's campaign staff invest in "looser underwear." In debates, Wellstone replied to Boschwitz's lectures about supply-side economics with a stinging one-liner: "What you just heard is a bunch of Boschwitz."

An Upset Victory

When Wellstone began his campaign, he seemed like the longest of long shots, but by Election Day he was a senator-elect. Here is how it all unfolded.

On the Sunday before the election, Boschwitz, one of the

most prominent Jews in Congress and a steadfast supporter of Israel, sent out a letter to the Twin Cities' Jewish community criticizing the Jewish Wellstone for not raising his children as Jews. The letter, which was signed by over fifty Boschwitz supporters, most of whom did not know its content, pointed out that both candidates in the race were Jewish. "But from there on the difference between them is profound," the letter said. "One, Paul Wellstone, has no connection with the Jewish community or our communal way of life. His children were brought up as non-Jews. . . . Everyone who knows Rudy knows that he is very family oriented and justly proud of his family." The implication was clear—Boschwitz was a better Jew than Wellstone.

Boschwitz badly misjudged the impact of the letter. Recipients of the letter were overwhelmingly opposed to what they perceived as an attack on Wellstone's Jewishness. "For one Jew to question the Jewishness of another Jew is something that is totally inappropriate," said one recipient. "It is something the worst anti-Semite wouldn't do."[26] A prominent rabbi called the letter "shameful," and another said it "ran contrary to everything we as a [Jewish] community have stood for."[27] The fallout had to have devastated Boschwitz. He was one of Congress's most steadfast supporters of Israel and was a major promoter of Jewish causes. Yet he came under withering criticism from within the Jewish community—including many of his Republican friends. Worse, the attack reinforced a theme of Wellstone's campaign that must have been especially irksome to Boschwitz: that the race was a David versus Goliath battle, with Wellstone filling the role of David—an enduring symbol of Jewish identity.

It wasn't just in the Jewish community that the letter backfired. Minnesotans had a history of rejecting negative campaigning, and Boschwitz's move violated the state's tradition of "Minnesota Nice." Not incidentally, the state is overwhelmingly Christian, and Wellstone's response reminded voters that the senator was launching an attack on Wellstone's decision about whom to marry. "I guess the senator is criticizing me for marrying a Christian," Wellstone said. The media also turned decisively against Boschwitz, depicting him as a bully who panicked as his campaign began sinking. "The warm and cuddly Boschwitz of the opening months of the campaign has disappeared," wrote a Twin Cities columnist. "That friend of Minnesota' has been replaced by a mean-spirited man who is proving that he's willing to do anything to win his Senate race against Paul Wellstone."[28]

With three days remaining before the election, the letter gave Wellstone the type of momentum that most political campaigns can only dream of. On the evening it was made public, a poll was released that showed Boschwitz holding a nine-point lead. But the Jewish letter quickly eclipsed all other issues in the campaign, and his lead evaporated. Boschwitz's press secretary later said, "We got about fifty calls from people who said they would switch their votes. They weren't crackpots either. They left their names. All of a sudden we could feel it slipping away."[29]

In the final three days of the campaign, Wellstone's superior grass-roots organization kicked in. Thousands of committed volunteers filled get-out-the-vote phone banks, distributed campaign literature, and stood in the biting cold, waving green Wellstone signs on traffic intersections. Wellstone himself campaigned at a frenzied pace, flying across the state for a final push that ended with him shaking hands in downtown Minneapolis until the polls closed. For his part, Boschwitz had stopped campaigning the night before and spent Election Day with two Senate colleagues, dining at an exclusive restaurant and preparing to savor another victory.

It was not to be. Hours later, the election results were in. Wellstone defeated Boschwitz 50.5 percent to 47.9 percent. He was the only challenger in the country to beat an incumbent senator in 1990. When told by a reporter that he had won, he looked dazed. "I did?" he asked.

Wellstone's evolution from community organizer to elected official was complete. With a controversial past, virtually no money, and a decidedly unsenatorial style, he had defeated an entrenched incumbent by employing the organizational techniques that he first learned from Saul Alinsky. By any measure, it was an extraordinary victory and represented a personal triumph for Wellstone. But as he celebrated his victory long into the night, a daunting realization also occurred to him: suddenly, he was a U.S. senator.

4

Faltering and Recovering

To be sure, mere passion, however genuinely felt, is not enough.

ON THE MORNING of November 6, 1990, Paul Wellstone appeared at a morning press conference and committed the first of several postcampaign blunders. Visibly exhausted from the previous night's celebration, he spoke disjointedly about his plans for the transition and then made a statement that he would later regret. "I want to give this all that I have," he said. "That means giving it 12 years, two terms. That is my post-campaign promise."[1] It was a politically unnecessary move—a poll later showed that Minnesota voters were indifferent to the promise—and it would prove to be a major liability when he decided in 2001 to run for a third term. It also exemplified Wellstone's tendency to speak before thinking about the consequences of his words. The decision was impulsive; he had not mentioned the pledge in the campaign and had never discussed it with his aides. If he had, they almost certainly would have advised him against it.

Even before Wellstone was sworn in, he was off on the wrong foot. A week after his first press conference, when asked by reporters how he would get along with archconservative North Carolina senator Jesse Helms, whom he had first encountered as a student at the University of North Carolina, he responded bluntly, "I have detested him since I was 19." Attempting to clarify his remarks several days later, Wellstone was unrepentant. "I didn't say hate. I said despised," he explained. "I have tremendous respect for the institution of the United States Senate. But the fact that I respect the institution does not mean that I need to respect the racists in the institution."[2] Asked if he was concerned that such a comment was a breach of the Senate's long-standing courtesy of not speaking ill of another senator, he responded, "I don't know, but I don't care. It's just the truth. I don't think Minnesotans expect me to come to the United States Senate and get involved in back-room deals with Jesse Helms."[3] The comments about Helms made the national news and raised questions about his ability to get along with his colleagues.

But Wellstone did not care about getting along with other senators. He went to Washington determined to use Saul Alinsky's quintessential organizing tool—conflict—as leverage with his colleagues. It was a strategy that had worked for him throughout his life—as a young professor fighting to save his job, as an organizer working with farmers and laborers, and as a long-shot candidate running for Senate—and Wellstone saw no reason to alter his style after his election. To the contrary, he viewed his victory as a mandate to shake up the Senate, not to make friends. He went to Washington as a party crasher, assuming that Alinsky's rules for organizing would work as a framework for governing.

He was wrong.

Within weeks of his election, Wellstone would face his first political crisis: the impending war in the Persian Gulf. When Saddam Hussein's Iraqi army invaded Kuwait six months earlier, President George H. W. Bush threatened military action against Saddam unless the troops were removed. Saddam refused, and Bush succeeded in assembling a broad international coalition to help the United States liberate Kuwait. War was imminent, and it was a problem for Wellstone. During the campaign, he had supported the buildup of military forces in Saudi Arabia as a deterrent to further Iraqi aggression but argued that economic sanctions against Iraq were preferable to the use of force.

Wellstone's position was hardly radical—at the time, the national debate was revolving around the question of whether the international community should impose economic sanctions against Iraq or intervene immediately— but as the possibility of war grew in the winter of 1990, he gained attention for his vocal opposition to the war. He grew increasingly critical of the White House and tried repeatedly to confront members of the administration about what he perceived to be their rush to war. In late November, he attended a reception at the White House held for new members of Congress and chose the occasion to discuss the war with President Bush. During a receiving line exchange, Wellstone told the president that the country "would be ripped apart" if it went to war. He then delivered the same message to the White House chief of staff, John Sununu, and the national security adviser, Brent Scowcroft, and gave them a letter inviting Bush to attend the town hall meetings he was holding in Minnesota. It was an unlikely setting for a confrontational exchange, and Wellstone's brazenness irked the president, prompting him to ask one of his advisers, in a comment overheard by a reporter and widely reported in the media, "Who is this chickenshit?"[4]

In the following weeks, Wellstone continued to alienate the Washington establishment with his criticism of the war. He accused the White House of pursuing a foreign policy that would lead to "mass slaughter" and criticized his fellow Democrats for not speaking out more strongly against the war. Then came the disastrous first week of January, when he confronted Vice President Dan Quayle during his swearing-in ceremony by handing Quayle an audiotape on which Minnesotans expressed opposition to the war. Days later, he held the controversial press conference at the Vietnam Veterans Memorial Wall. When military operations finally began, he violated a basic political rule that says once war breaks out opponents should temper their criticism out of respect for American soldiers. Wellstone's self-righteousness grated on his colleagues, angered his constituents, and gave the media an easy story line—the meteoric rise and sudden fall of an upstart politician.

Wellstone would write in his autobiography, *The Conscience of a Liberal,* "It was a horrible beginning! I wanted to find a hole in the ground and disappear."[5]

Mathews's Rules for Governing

If there was a single lesson that Wellstone could have learned from his difficult entry into the Senate, it was that he pulled the wrong book off his shelf when framing his approach to governing. Instead of applying Saul Alinsky's rules for radicals, he should have referenced a book that he knew equally well: *U.S. Senators and Their World*, written by a former professor at the University of North Carolina, Donald Mathews. Written in 1959, the book is still considered one of the most influential and accurate descriptions of Senate customs. In it, Mathews describes the inner workings of the Senate club—an environment governed by what he calls "norms and folkways." The Senate, he explains, is founded on the principles of trust, tradition, and respect. Friendships often matter more than ideology and partisanship; the best senators are those who build strong interpersonal relationships with their colleagues. According to Mathews, the ideal senator is a legislative workhorse who specializes in one or two policy areas and serves a long apprenticeship before asserting himself. To be effective, a newly elected member must maintain a low profile, defer to his more senior colleagues, and wait patiently before delivering his first floor speech.[6]

Wellstone knew this book intimately. He studied under Mathews after it was published, assigned it to his classes at Carleton, and borrowed its title for one of the chapters of his autobiography. He knew that it reflected more than just an academic theory of legislative behavior, because he was familiar with the wide body of literature that supported its conclusions. Yet it was not until later in his career that he came to truly appreciate its prescience. In *The Conscience of a Liberal*, he wrote, "It is amazing how much of what happens in the Senate is based on what Donald R. Mathews, in his pioneering book, . . . calls 'norms and folkways.'"[7]

When he first arrived in Washington, why did Wellstone ignore the lessons he had learned from Mathews and taught to his students? He knew better than to enter the Senate with such bluster and carelessness, and yet he seemed to believe that the norms and folkways applied to everyone but him. With a proclivity for talking first and thinking later, he did the precise opposite of what Donald Mathews said a newly elected senator must do to succeed. Where the prototypical senator was measured and deferential, Wellstone was loud and impulsive. He applied Alinsky instead of applying Mathews.

It was after this choppy start that Wellstone began to realize that if he did not soften his style he would become a marginal figure in the Senate. He began listening to the advice of former and current senators, who suggested ways to gain the respect of his colleagues and become more effective. Walter Mondale, whose presidential candidacy Wellstone had worked against in 1984 but whom he now considered a mentor, told Wellstone to be patient. "Remember," Mondale recalled telling Wellstone, "you don't have to ram the doors down now, you have a key to the door, you're a senator."[8] Republicans such as Orrin Hatch from Utah and Ted Stevens from Alaska suggested ways to stand firm against opponents without losing credibility. Democrats Howell Heflin, Tom Harkin, and James Exon gave Wellstone fatherly advice about how to get along with colleagues.

The liberal Paul Simon quickly became Wellstone's best friend in the Senate, offering him reassurances when Wellstone took difficult votes or made rookie mistakes. Simon counseled him to avoid turf battles with other liberals and to allow himself to enjoy his experiences. Simon also taught Wellstone that he could be a forceful and effective advocate as long as he demonstrated respect for both his colleagues and the institution of the Senate. "I think sometimes Paul [Simon] didn't appreciate enough the importance of conflict," Wellstone wrote in his autobiography. "But he reminded me of the critical distinction between disagreement and destruction."[9]

Despite Wellstone's foot-in-mouth tendency, he grew on his colleagues. With his frizzy hair and disheveled oversized suits, he was a refreshing presence in the Senate club. He rediscovered his self-deprecating sense of humor, learned to control his self-righteousness, and built lasting friendships.

Assembling a Team

Wellstone also began to assemble a seasoned team. Initially, he filled key policy positions in his Washington office with people who had backgrounds similar to his own—progressive activists with organizing experience. But his controversial press conference caused Wellstone to rethink his hiring strategy. "The Wall incident was I think a wake-up call for Paul that he needed people who were more seasoned, less campaign oriented, more attuned to the presentation of a senator—people who might have said, 'Paul don't do that,'" said former chief of staff Colin McGinnis.[10] Finding trustworthy and experienced Hill staffers proved easier than Wellstone might have imagined.

In the summer of 1991, a short, middle-aged Senate staffer named Mike Epstein approached Paul and Sheila while they were on a walk on Capitol Hill. Epstein, who had spent the preceding two decades becoming one of the Senate's most knowledgeable aides, had been watching Wellstone closely. While he admired the freshman senator's idealism, Epstein knew that if Wellstone did not soften his style he would be an ineffective lawmaker. During the conversation Epstein said to Wellstone, "You need a legislative director," and offered to do the job.[11] Wellstone hired him on the spot. They became instant friends and shared much in common—similar ages, religious backgrounds, and a sense of idealism. According to Wellstone, in their first encounter Epstein told him, "I've been here for thirty years and I still believe in changing the world." Yet Epstein and Wellstone had taken dramatically different paths in pursuit of their ideals. While Wellstone had been raising havoc as an organizer in rural Minnesota, Epstein was becoming a master insider in one of the nation's most powerful institutions.

In addition to bringing in Epstein to run his legislative activities, Wellstone also recognized that he needed someone to run his office well. It was a critical realization that reflected Wellstone's capacity to admit his own weaknesses and to look to others to compensate for them. By his own admission, he was a terrible manager. In addition to being prone to make impulsive decisions, he sometimes lost his temper and was a demanding boss. Intensely competitive and driven, he regularly called his aides early in the morning with complaints about news coverage or ideas about his legislative and political agenda. "The biggest tension was that everything that dealt with Minnesota and dealt with fighting for the underdog and fighting for real people, was a priority," recalled former aide Josh Syrjamaki. "Paul would have these meetings with the staff where he would say, our number priority is education and children, healthcare, race and poverty and gender issues, the environment, prescription drugs, veterans, economic development, fighting for steelworkers, working for farmers. So before you knew it, we were at 12, 13, 14, 15 priorities."[12]

Knowing that he needed to tighten the office's scope of work, Wellstone hired another former student, Kari Moe, as his chief of staff in the fall of 1991. Moe had been a student leader in the effort to save Wellstone's job at Carleton, and the two had maintained a close friendship ever since. After graduating from Carleton, Moe moved to Chicago and

worked as a top aide to Mayor Harold Washington. Experienced, loyal, and focused, Moe would lead Wellstone's office through his chaotic first term. Her leadership, combined with Epstein's legislative experience, positioned Wellstone to start winning legislative victories.

Finding a Focus

Epstein's first piece of advice to Wellstone could have been taken from a page out of Donald Mathews's book: focus on a single area and make it your specialty. While it was good advice, Wellstone's options were not readily apparent. Although health care had been a central theme in Wellstone's campaign, it was already a major issue in Congress, and senators like Ted Kennedy claimed it as theirs. Other issues important to Wellstone, such as the economy, environment, and agriculture, were too broad and high profile. Fiscal and budgetary matters held little interest for him, and he was too impatient to focus on low-profile subjects.

The issue of government reform was another story. Wellstone cared passionately about holding Congress more accountable and changing the relationship between campaign donors and elected officials. He wanted to open the doors of the Senate club and throw light on the relationship between special interests and members of Congress. By most measures, the issue was a perfect fit—he was already identified as a reformer, and few other senators had claimed reform as "their" issue. But it was also risky. By definition, he would be trying to force his colleagues to change their behavior and, in some cases, to end long-standing traditions that governed the relationship between them and special interests. Wellstone was working to improve relationships with his colleagues; pushing reform would likely mean alienating and annoying the very people on which his success as a senator depended.

But he pushed ahead anyway, focusing first on finding ways to limit the influence of lobbying groups. He told friends that, when he arrived in the Senate, he realized that even he had underestimated the influence that lobbyists had not only on the voting behavior of individual members but also on how the Senate as an institution operates. Even his like-minded colleagues seemed resigned to the fact that lobbyists and interest groups held enormous influence over the behavior of senators from both parties. Wellstone said he was scandalized by the political tone of the weekly Democratic caucus meetings and criticized his fellow Democrats for trying to find ways to avoid issues that would alienate key constituencies and donors instead of pushing the issues they cared about.

In April 1992, Wellstone had an opportunity to take action. He was on the floor of the Senate as it finished a late-night debate over proposed legislation that would have provided a $25 billion bailout to the struggling S&L industry, which had been shaken by a series of high-profile scandals. The bailout was highly controversial and viewed by many as a reward for corporate malfeasance. But it was strongly supported by the banking and S&L industry, which argued that the bill was necessary in order to avoid an economic crisis. A clear majority of senators supported the bailout, but few of them wanted to go on record as such. So when the Senate debate ended, Majority Leader George Mitchell, a Democrat, called for a voice vote, a long-standing and unwritten Senate tradition that allows individual senators to not go on record on controversial legislation.

Wellstone was expecting the move and immediately rose

to object. He believed that voice voting was simply a way for members of Congress to have it both ways with their constituents— senators could support a piece of unpopular legislation in the Senate and simply tell their constituents that they opposed it. Not surprisingly, the maneuver irked Wellstone's colleagues. In his autobiography, he recalled a "wave" of senators walking up to him on the Senate floor, insisting that he back down. As one newspaper columnist wrote at the time, "They came singly and in pairs, and they were seething. Some of them used four-letter words. What the four-letter-word do you think you're doing? Why do you look under rocks for trouble? Take a walk. This is grandstand stuff."[13] The pressure served only to make Wellstone deepen his resolve. "All the guys coming to him on the floor pleading with him to step back made him dig in his heels more," said Colin McGinnis. Wellstone insisted on the recorded vote, and he defiantly voted *for* the legislation in an effort to show his colleagues that "my greater principals are reform and accountability."

Despite angering some of his colleagues, Wellstone received a political lift from the S&L vote. The incident was widely covered by the Minnesota press; he was praised for standing up to his fellow senators and for delivering on one of his key campaign promises: pushing for greater government accountability. Back in Minnesota, people shouted, "Give ']em hell, Paul"; one columnist wrote a story that headlined "True News Flash: A Politician Keeps a Promise."[14] Wellstone also found that the fallout from his fellow senators was surprisingly mild. By holding his ground, he earned the respect of his colleagues. A senator who had strenuously lobbied Wellstone to back down later approached him on the floor, patted his back, and said, "Son, you did right."[15]

Wellstone Hits His Stride

By the end of his second year in Washington, Wellstone had made significant progress in refurbishing his image among his constituents and the press. His approval ratings nudged above 50 percent, and the Minnesota media began reporting about his transformation into a serious player in the Senate. For example, a long article headlined "New Gains by a New Wellstone" was published in January 1993 in the Minneapolis-based *Star Tribune* and described Wellstone as "an emerging force to be reckoned with." The article portrays a senator who used persistence and charm to transform himself from a career protester to an effective lawmaker and popular politician. "He has been on a nonstop mission to convince citizens that his system-rattling politics are in their interest, or, failing that, to get them to at least like him as a person." Wellstone's efforts were the result, the article concluded, of a three-part approach: "He's fought to control his own energy, passionate idealism and sensitive ego. He's struggled to accomplish something in the Senate without selling out. And he's tried to keep in contact with his liberal-labor coalition in Minnesota while winning over other Minnesotans."[16]

In the spring of 1993, his efforts continued to pay off, as he pushed a legislative agenda defined by the issue of government reform. That spring he joined with Senator Carl Levin, a liberal Democrat from Michigan, in sponsoring a bill that sought to plug loopholes in existing lobbying laws to assure that all lobbyists are registered and to improve enforcement of the rules. Levin viewed the modest bill as the first step in accomplishing the larger goal of banning the practice of gift giving by lobbyists to members of Congress and their staffs. Wellstone, who had grown close to

Levin, shared his friend's incremental approach but wanted a provision added to the bill that would require lobbyists to fully disclose their gift-giving activities. When the bill came to the floor of the Senate in May 1993, Wellstone added an amendment that said that gifts exceeding a value of fifty dollars a year given by a lobbyist to a member of Congress or his or her staff must be disclosed. This included meals, entertainment, and travel—all of which were routinely provided by lobbying groups without disclosure. Levin preferred an outright ban on gifts and believed the amendment would weaken momentum for a gift ban, but Wellstone persisted and, after accepting some minor modifications, forced the Senate to vote on the proposal. Although many senators had little interest in exposing their relationships with lobbyists, the proposal passed handily.

It was a huge victory. Two days later, the *New York Times* ran an editorial titled "The Wellspring of Lobby Reform," which praised Wellstone for his persistence in passing the amendment. "All it takes is one good man or woman," the editorial began. "In this case, the good man is Senator Paul Wellstone, a Senate outsider who's one of its most idealistic members."[17] Moreover, the lobby disclosure amendment generated momentum for an outright gift ban. Although the House version of the lobby disclosure bill was held up and ultimately killed by Speaker Tom Foley, Wellstone and Senator Frank Lautenberg of New Jersey introduced a comprehensive gift ban in the Senate. The bill called for a forthright ban on gifts of meals, travel, and entertainment given to members of Congress by lobbyists. Although the legislation stalled in committee for the remainder of 1993, by the next spring it was up for consideration by the full Senate and passed in May 1994.

Making Amends with Veterans

As Wellstone was making his mark as a legislator, he also took a series of extraordinary steps to improve his relationship with the veterans he had so deeply offended with his ill-advised press conference at the Vietnam Veterans Memorial in 1991. "Paul should not have done the press conference," said former campaign manager and state director Jeff Blodgett. "Veterans groups are mostly focused on what happens to veterans once they get home, so they were not necessarily Paul's opponents by any means. But when he went to the memorial, it raised the ire of all the veterans' groups, particularly the Vietnam vets."[18] Wellstone was devastated. "I never should have held a press conference at or anywhere near this sacred memorial," he wrote in his autobiography. "I wanted to dramatize the dangers of military action. Instead, I deeply hurt many Vietnam Veterans, really all of the veterans' community."[19]

Wellstone set out to make amends with veterans, starting with an apology. Shortly after the press conference, his office set up public meetings with veterans throughout Minnesota, where he apologized for his insensitivity and listened to their grievances. "Paul was very touched, and he learned as he listened to their stories and to the struggles that veterans had," said Josh Syrjamaki, who served as Wellstone's liaison to the veterans' community.[20] Wellstone discovered that the issues affecting veterans were similar to those facing the people he had spent a lifetime organizing. He found a tight-knit community of men (and some women) who had experienced indescribable tragedy in service to their country yet had been largely forgotten when they returned home. They suffered from inadequate health care, debilitating mental illnesses in some cases, and, above all, the indifference of government officials.

To rebuild his relationship with veterans, Wellstone assigned several staff members to serve as liaisons to veterans' groups. "There were several different ways that we would go out and listen to veterans and find out what was happening in their lives," said Josh Syrjamaki, who led the efforts. "One of them was just to answer the phone calls and letters of veterans. The other way was old-fashioned Wellstone community organizing. We would travel throughout the state and we would convene community discussions with veterans. Paul would simply sit down and say, tell me what's going on in your lives. What can I do? How can I be helpful? And a million ideas would come at him and usually throughout the conversations, we'd be able to distill it down to 2 or 3 projects to work on."[21]

Back in Washington, Wellstone worked to act on the stories he heard from veterans at home. He joined the Senate Veterans' Affairs Committee and began lobbying vigorously on behalf of veterans. After hearing about a group of Minnesota veterans who had been unknowingly exposed to atomic energy testing by the U.S. government in the 1950s, he demanded a government investigation and passed legislation to compensate the veterans, who became known as the "Atomic Veterans." He became deeply involved in efforts to compensate veterans who had been exposed to Agent Orange in Vietnam. Wellstone also worked to improve the quality of health-care services delivered by the Veterans Administration and engaged in heated debates over appropriations funding for veterans' health care. The efforts paid off. By the end of Wellstone's first term, he had received awards from the Vietnam Veterans of America, the Paralyzed Veterans of America, the Disabled American Veterans, and the Military Order of the Purple Heart.

After a difficult start, Wellstone could claim an impressive record of accomplishments for a freshman senator. He had delivered on a campaign promise to reform the way the Senate operates, built friendships with members of both parties, and forged an unlikely alliance with the same veterans' groups that had once bitterly denounced him. He had learned from his mistakes and grown into an effective legislator. But while he had made great progress as a senator, he also began worrying about his next great challenge: winning reelection.

The Republicans' Number One Target

In the fall of 1994, the Democratic Party was pounded in the midterm congressional elections. The Republicans, led by the bombastic new Speaker of the House, Newt Gingrich, regained majorities in both houses of Congress with a campaign manifesto called the Contract With America. The contract read like a handbook for conservatives: tax cuts, term limits, restrictions on immigration, benefit cuts to welfare recipients, and increased defense spending. The Republican victories were decisive and overwhelming, knocking the Democrats and President Clinton on their heels. Back in Minnesota, the Republican Party held a triumphant election night victory party, with the activists gleefully chanting, "Wellstone's next!"

Although many Democrats were despondent and sullen, Wellstone was energized. He believed the Republicans would overreach their mandate with an agenda that was too extreme for average voters. He insisted that the Democratic Party and the progressives fight the Republican majority with every possible effort. "We will not roll over! This isn't a Contract With America," Wellstone shouted to party activists on election night. "It's a Contract On America, and I'll be on the floor with amendments, I'm going to take this Contract on, and we're going to defeat this extremist agenda!"

True to his word, Wellstone spent the next two years as a constant presence on the floor of the Senate. In nearly every legislative debate regarding the Contract With America, he used parliamentary procedures to block, amend, or delay the Republican majority. In the process, he perfected his law-making skills, mastering the technique of objecting to unanimous consent agreements. "To have power in the Senate," Wellstone later wrote, "you need to know only two words: *I object.*" He used the objection constantly, and although he lost many of the battles, he emerged as one of the leading critics of the Contract With America.

Given Wellstone's fierce opposition to the contract, it was hardly surprising that a leaked memo from the national Republican Party identified Wellstone as the top target for defeat in 1996. As early as 1993, the Minnesota Republican Party began to wage a vigorous campaign against him, publishing the newsletter "The Wellstone Watch," which lampooned Wellstone with mocking articles and cartoon drawings depicting him as pot-bellied and disheveled. Immediately after the 1994 elections, the state Republican Party chairman began holding weekly news conferences, attacking him for everything from not paying taxes on his famed green bus to breaking a promise to not accept political action committee (PAC) money. When they ran out of issues, they sent out press releases with memorable headlines like "Paul Wellstone Is a Lying, Hypocritical Whiner."

While Republican Party officials thrashed Wellstone, his former rival prepared for another campaign.

The Rematch

From as early as two days following his 1990 defeat, Rudy Boschwitz made clear his interest in taking his Senate seat back from Paul Wellstone. Passing up a 1994 opportunity to run for the seat left open by retiring Republican senator Dave Durenburger, Boschwitz set out to defeat the man who had humiliated him. Despite his advancing age and frail appearance, Boschwitz plunged into the campaign with single-minded intensity. He immediately focused on Wellstone, ignoring and then easily defeating a state legislator for the Republican Party endorsement.

Boschwitz had a simple campaign message: Wellstone was too liberal for Minnesota. The Boschwitz campaign hired a conservative political consultant named Arthur Finkelstein, an architect of the strategy of labeling an opponent, simply and relentlessly, a liberal. For this campaign, Finkelstein devised a campaign message that Boschwitz would repeat nearly every time he uttered Wellstone's name: "Paul Wellstone is embarrassingly liberal." Boschwitz ran television advertisements implying that Wellstone was a pot-smoking throwback to the 1960s, a coddler of violent criminals, and an opponent of requiring welfare recipients to work.

When the Senate began debating President Clinton's welfare reform bill in August 1996, Boschwitz sought to capitalize on a potential political opening. The bill, which required welfare recipients to seek jobs and ended benefits for legal immigrants and children, was a centerpiece of Clinton's effort to portray himself as a new type of Democrat. With public opinion overwhelmingly supportive of the bill, it became a hot-button political issue, and intense pressure mounted on Wellstone to vote for it. Yet Wellstone had deep reservations about the bill. He supported the work requirement provision but was adamantly opposed to cutting off children and legal immigrants from public assistance. Despite the political risks, he voted against the legislation, one of only twelve other senators and the only one up for reelection to do so. "Many of Paul's colleagues came up to him and said, 'It's been nice knowing you,'" said former chief of staff Kari Moe. "They called it Paul's political suicide vote."[22] Boschwitz was thrilled. In debates and in his campaign materials, he referred to Wellstone as "Senator Welfare" and lambasted the senator for being outside the mainstream of Minnesota voters.

Wellstone responded vigorously to the Boschwitz attacks. His campaign immediately released a television ad in which he explained his reasons for voting against the welfare bill. "I will not vote for a bill that puts more children in poverty," he said. "My parents taught me to stand up for what I believe in and to do what I think is right."[23] He ignored Boschwitz's charges that he was a liberal, since Minnesota voters already knew that anyway. Instead, Wellstone went on a counteroffensive. He knew, from both his personal encounters with voters and from polling data, that while many Minnesotans disagreed with his positions on issues, they respected him for being honest and for making his positions clear to them. In his speeches and advertisements, he sought to drive that point home. He proudly defended his record, including the welfare reform vote. He also relied on a simple message of economic populism: "The pharmaceutical companies, drug companies and oil companies might not like me very much. But they already have great representation. It's the rest of the people that need it."

Wellstone also vigorously attacked Boschwitz as being out of touch and too conservative. By then, Newt Gingrich had gone too far with his conservative agenda and provided a perfect foil for Wellstone and other Democrats. He blasted Boschwitz as a Gingrich extremist, using the former senator's twelve-year voting record as evidence. He also used Boschwitz's negative campaign and his own designation as the Republicans' top target to portray himself again as an underdog. Wellstone ended his stump speech with the following words: "When they make me the number one target, they make working families and children their number one target. I'm the top target, but that's not the price I pay, it's the privilege I've earned!"

Angering the Base

But Wellstone would pay a price with some of his staunchest supporters in the summer of 1996. Despite his unapologetically liberal positions on issues and his relentless opposition to the Gingrich agenda, he was confronted with an election-year conundrum. In June, he unexpectedly announced plans to vote for a Republican-sponsored bill called "The Defense of Marriage Act." The legislation, known by its acronym DOMA, was a creative ploy by Republicans to drive a wedge into the Democratic base—if Democrats voted against the legislation, they would be accused of being out of the mainstream, but if they voted for it, they would anger their gay and lesbian supporters. The bill defined marriage strictly as the union of a man and a woman, effectively criminalizing gay marriage at the federal level. Supported by the Clinton White House and a vast majority of senators of both parties, the legislation put Wellstone in a particularly difficult position. Under withering attack for being too liberal, he risked alienating voters in Minnesota—a clear majority of whom supported the ban—by voting against the bill. But voting for the bill would put him at odds with his liberal base and would alienate members of the gay and lesbian community, many of whom considered Wellstone a hero.

For Wellstone, the decision was further complicated by his own beliefs. As a longtime advocate for human rights and as a staunch supporter of gays and lesbians (until then he had been considered the Senate's leading gay rights advocate), he understood why opponents of the legislation viewed the bill as an assault on their civil liberties. But as a decidedly conventional man in his personal life, whose notion of marriage was defined by his own traditional marriage and lifestyle, he was uncomfortable with the idea of same-sex marriage. Once it was thrust onto the political agenda, Wellstone felt that he had no choice but to make what would become the one vote he later said he regretted. After announcing his support of the legislation on a talk radio show—without having informed his aides or alerted gay and lesbian leaders—he was roundly criticized by his liberal supporters. At a fund-raiser for the gay and lesbian community planned coincidentally for the day after he announced his decision, he was met with angry, tearful supporters who felt profoundly betrayed.

The decision to vote for DOMA was widely viewed as a politically expedient way for Wellstone to get out of a tough vote. But the reality was more complicated. The truth was that Wellstone had deep reservations about allowing same-sex marriage. He had never felt comfortable with homosexuality, having grown up in a socially conservative environment. While the decision was personally devastating—he was upset with himself for mishandling the announcement and regretted the pain he had caused—it reflected Wellstone's beliefs at the time. He told his disappointed supporters that he needed to "be educated about the issue," and over time, he was. In his autobiography, Wellstone admitted that he had doubts about his decision. "What troubles me is that as a U.S. senator, I may not have cast the right vote on DOMA," he wrote. "I am proud of my reputation for always voting for what I believe in, regardless of the political consequences, but what if I rationalized my vote by making myself believe this was my honest position?"[24] But many of Wellstone's confidantes believe that, in reality, it was, in fact, his honest position.

To some of his liberal supporters, Wellstone's vote on DOMA reflected what they saw as his gradual selling out to Washington. He was no longer the fire-breathing liberal out to poke Washington in the eye. He had changed, and some of his core supporters from the first campaign felt let down. This was in some measure Wellstone's own doing—by setting himself up as a damn-the-torpedoes progressive, any toning down of his style would be bound to anger some elements of his base. He had set high expectations for himself—that he would be an effective senator who could also lead a national renewal of progressive politics. Then reality intervened, and Wellstone found that he had more than his hands full with his work as a senator—both as a legislator in Washington and as a provider of constituent services back home—and he had been forced to moderate his goals.

Fighting Back and Winning

While some viewed Wellstone's transformation as evidence of a sellout, others saw it as a reflection of his maturation as a politician. No longer an unknown candidate with no money, he was a sitting U.S. senator with a national base of supporters and an impressive ability to raise large sums of money in small donations. Although he still inspired passion in his supporters (despite the DOMA controversy, Wellstone's campaign galvanized an enormous and highly energized base), he wanted his second Senate campaign to reflect his accomplishments and hit back hard against his Republican opponents. He had no interest in presenting himself to voters using the same formula as his first Senate race, when he was depicted as a quirky college professor with no money.

Wellstone and his advisers clashed with Bill Hillsman, the creator of his unorthodox 1990 ads who was rehired to do the 1996 ads. Hillsman wanted to create groundbreaking and light-hearted spots, including one in which Wellstone was to be portrayed as Godzilla, taking fire from all sides. Instead of responding to the attacks directly, Hillsman wanted to make fun of the opposition. Since the 1990 victory, Hillsman had gone on to build a national reputation for his creative ads, but he also developed a reputation among campaign strategists as being politically tone-deaf and stubbornly arrogant. Hillsman was often viewed as being less interested in electing candidates than in raising his profile and growing his advertising business.

By the end of the summer in 1996, Wellstone's relationship with Hillsman had deteriorated. Refusing to produce ads consistent with Wellstone's wishes, Hillsman was fired and replaced by Mandy Grunwald, a seasoned political consultant who had worked on Bill Clinton's 1992 campaign. "When I was hired in 1996, the campaign was not prepared to deal with the attacks that it was under," Grunwald said. "He felt that he wasn't fighting back in the way he needed to. And when he hired me he said, 'I think I need something different.'"[25] Grunwald produced ads that showed Wellstone speaking directly into the camera and talking about his record and that depicted him as a hard-working senator who delivered results for the people of the state. While hardly groundbreaking, the ads were highly effective. After the election was over, a Republican campaign operative told a former Wellstone staffer, "We knew the campaign was over when you fired Hillsman and hired Grunwald."

The ads, combined with Wellstone's aggressive grassroots campaign strategy, succeeded in convincing Minnesotans that Wellstone was still an outsider but that he had become effective working on the inside. Polls taken in the fall of 1996 showed that Wellstone's lead was widening and that the Republican attack ads had gone too far. Although Wellstone ran hard-hitting ads contrasting his record with Boschwitz's, voters overwhelmingly blamed the Republicans for the campaign's nasty tone and seemed underwhelmed by the assertion that Wellstone was a liberal. If Minnesotans knew one thing about Wellstone—and they had known it for as long as he had been in the public eye—it was that he was a liberal. They accepted the fact that he was a liberal, because they knew that he was straightforward and honest. "So the Republicans are saying I'm a liberal," Wellstone said during the campaign. "Yeah, well what else is new?"

As the campaign entered the homestretch, Rudy Boschwitz grew increasingly desperate. Facing another humiliating loss to his nemesis, he resorted to a familiar tactic. On the Friday before Election Day, six years to the day after he had sent the infamous "Jewish letter" accusing Wellstone of being a bad Jew, Boschwitz held a press conference at the state capitol. Surrounded by a group of veterans, he accused Wellstone of having burned an American flag during a protest at UNC. The charge was a complete fabrication: Boschwitz had no evidence, no witnesses, and no other information about the alleged flag-burning incident. The attack backfired. The media pounced on Boschwitz's failure to produce any evidence, and the Wellstone campaign countered with its own press conference featuring dozens of decorated war veterans, including leaders of several veterans' groups, demanding an apology. The campaign was over.

In the end, Wellstone won decisively, by nine percentage points. After hitting the ground stumbling, he had regrouped, found his stride as a senator, and coasted to reelection.

5

A Successful Second Term

Politics is a strong and slow boring of
hard boards. It takes both passion and
perspective.

BY THE END of 1996, Wellstone had estab-
lished a level of credibility that seemed unattainable six
years earlier. He had matured as a lawmaker during his first
term and proved his durability as a politician by winning
reelection decisively. He had built strong friendships among
his colleagues and learned to pick his legislative battles
wisely, to compromise when necessary, and to respect the
institution of the Senate. He also came to recognize that he
often appeared shrill and self-righteous, and he had made a
conscious effort to tone down in style. By outward appearance, he seemed a different person from the abrasive outsider he had been when he first came to the Senate.

But Wellstone demonstrated on the first day of his second
term in office that, while he had adjusted his style, some-

thing remained of his old confrontational style. It was a day of ceremony—the only items on the Senate's agenda were the swearing-in ceremonies of newly and reelected senators. By previous agreement, the Senate was set to recess until after the presidential inauguration two weeks later, but when Senate Majority Leader Trent Lott called for an adjournment at the end of the day's ceremonies, Wellstone rose to object. "Mr. President," he said, addressing the presiding officer of the Senate, "I feel very strongly, and I think that an overwhelming majority of people in the country feel, that there is no more important thing we can do than to pass a reform bill and get a lot of this big money out of politics. . . . I feel like we should not go into recess and we ought to get started on this. I wonder if the majority leader can make a commitment that within the first 100 days, we will at least have such a bill on the floor of the Senate."

It was a classic Wellstone maneuver. Once again, he had defied decorum and annoyed the leaders of both parties. Lott told Wellstone it was impossible for him to make a certain time commitment to consider campaign reform, and Senate Minority Leader Tom Daschle gently admonished him for raising the issue at a time when the leadership had agreed not to consider legislative business. But Wellstone was undeterred: "What about within the first four months as opposed to the first three months? Can the majority leader make a commitment that he will do everything possible to try to have a bill on the floor of the Senate within a four-month period? That is reasonable, and that is all I am asking for." After a long and tense exchange, Wellstone eventually dropped his objection, and the Senate adjourned.[1]

Not a day into his second term, Wellstone made it clear that his capacity for annoying his colleagues was undiminished.

Improbable Partnerships

If Wellstone excelled at irritating other senators, he also had a knack for getting them to like him. On the one hand, he employed the Senate's complex and often arcane rules to obstruct objectionable legislation and to promote his agenda, often to the chagrin of his colleagues. But he also reached out to his colleagues on a personal level and became a loyal friend to Republicans and Democrats alike. Unstintingly decent, he disarmed even his harshest critics with self-deprecation and used his charm to develop partnerships with even the most conservative Republicans.

Nothing was more unlikely than his friendship with Senator Jesse Helms. In 1990, Wellstone called Helms a racist and stated publicly that he "despised" the deeply conservative North Carolinian. But as Wellstone softened his partisan edge, he gradually took a liking to Helms. He noticed the way Helms interacted with the elevator operators, custodians, and other support staff at the Capitol. While many senators ignored these workers, Helms took time to acknowledge them with a greeting or complimentary remark. "One of the ways you judge a person," Wellstone said in praising Helms, "is just the way you watch them treat people. . . . I don't think there is anybody in the Senate who treats them with more grace and is kinder and more appreciative."[2]

Although the two senators were on opposing sides of the great majority of issues, they found a few issues on which they were in agreement. They coauthored legislation to sanction the Chinese government for human rights abuses and collaborated on issues of trade and globalization. In the process, they became friends. When Helms retired from the Senate, Wellstone paid him tribute on the floor of the Senate. To thank him, Helms sent Wellstone a handwritten letter addressed to "My dear Paul." After noting his appreciation for Wellstone's remarks, he wrote, "You're a principled senator who is willing to take a stand (as much as I may occasionally disagree with you)—and that's something seldom found in Washington these days."[3]

Helms was not the only Republican with whom Wellstone worked well. He coauthored with Senator Sam Brownback of Kansas legislation aimed at curtailing international sex trafficking. When it passed in 2000, it was hailed as a major victory in the effort to combat the growing practice of human trafficking—particularly of girls and women into forced prostitution. He also introduced legislation with Ohio Republican Mike DeWine called the Workforce Investment Act, a major overhaul of the federal government's job training program. It was signed into law by President Clinton and described by the Department of Labor as "the most exhaustive reform ever of the nation's employment and training delivery system."[4]

And then there was the Republican senator who was so deeply emotional when he was asked to comment on Wellstone's death—Pete Domenici of New Mexico. In politics and style, Domenici was as close to a polar opposite as Wellstone had in the U.S. Senate. Described by one journalist as "a gray, pragmatic fiscal and social conservative," Domenici is known as a savvy political deal maker and respected Senate insider who played an instrumental role in winning passage of President Ronald Reagan's 1986 landmark tax reform legislation.[5] In nearly every respect, the well-dressed and taciturn Domenici represented everything about the Washington establishment that Wellstone had spent a career fighting against.

Despite their differences, the two senators liked each other and shared common experiences that had transformed their lives. Domenici and his wife, Nancy, have a grown daughter who has struggled with mental illness for most of her life; Wellstone's brother, Stephen, has battled schizophrenia since the age of nineteen. Both senators had experienced the anguish of mental illness and the devastation the disease can have on families and loved ones. When their daughter was diagnosed, the Domenicis became immersed in the issue. "You get into the world of these dread diseases—you hear stories—they're terrible from the standpoint of what's happening to these people and what's happening to their families," Pete Domenici said. "Society was just ignoring them, denying them resources."[6] For Wellstone, that denial of resources amounted to discrimination against people with diseases that are no more avoidable— and no less treatable—than physical diseases like cancer.

Domenici and Wellstone quickly agreed that the most serious problem facing sufferers of mental illness is that insurance companies are not required by law to cover costs associated with the treatment of mental illness. As a result, sufferers of mental illness and their families are often left with impossible choices when confronted by the high costs of treatment: either pay for the services out of pocket or allow the disease to go untreated. The first choice can lead to financial ruin, as it did in the case of Wellstone's parents (who spent twenty years repaying the costs of Stephen's two-year hospitalization); the consequences of the second can be lethal.

Two years after Wellstone's election, the two senators teamed up to introduce legislation that would require insurance companies to offer the same coverage for mental illness as they do for other diseases, a concept known as parity. In 1996, after four years of pushing the bill, they succeeded in passing the Mental Health Parity Act, which was signed into law by President Clinton. The bill's passage was a major victory, but Wellstone and Domenici were disappointed that the final version allowed employers to shift the costs to employees by raising co-payments and deductibles on insurance policies. They immediately began crafting new, broader legislation that would apply what they termed "full parity" to the treatment of illnesses. Although it passed both houses of Congress in 2001, it was gutted in conference committee in favor of a one-year extension of the original bill. In 2002, the two senators reintroduced the bill, but it languished in Congress until the end of the year, when yet another one-year extension passed. In the wake of Wellstone's death, Domenici reintroduced the bill in the current Congress as the Paul Wellstone Mental Health Parity Act.

Despite the fact that the legislation has not yet been passed into law, Wellstone's alliance with Domenici is perhaps the most illuminating example of his personal growth in the Senate. Working with Domenici, Wellstone was at his best. He was passionate—he spoke emotionally and eloquently about his brother's experiences—but not sentimental. He was persistent and insisted on pushing forward in the face of repeated setbacks. He was persuasive, both in his advocacy of the legislation and in his efforts to push Domenici to take a more aggressive approach. And he was playful—when Domenici's assistant once asked Wellstone why he was calling for the senator, he responded, "Mental health! What the hell else do we agree on?"[7] Above all, what stood out in this unlikely alliance was Wellstone's love of politics and mastery of his vocation.

Wellstone's Rules

By the middle of Wellstone's second term, he was riding high. He was able to list a series of legislative accomplishments, and not just things that he blocked from making it through the Senate. He helped pass important elements of the Violence Against Women Act, passed the legislation with Senators Brownback and DeWine that was mentioned previously, passed dozens of amendments to farm bills, had a major impact on passing reform legislation, and won several awards for passing bills supporting veterans and veterans health services. But Wellstone did not limit his definition of effectiveness to passing legislation. "Paul genuinely believed that effectiveness could be measured in a variety of ways," said former chief of staff Colin McGinnis. "To be effective, you had to do a whole bunch of things at the same time: shock the place from outside, work on the inside to get things done, and hold up the work of people across the country who were doing great things—highlight what they were doing and draw attention to them."

McGinnis points to Wellstone's relationship to foreign policy as an example of how he became a more effective advocate of his positions, even if they were the same positions he held when first arriving in the Senate. "Early on, he did these hysterical, thrashing speeches on foreign policy, including his maiden speech in 1990 on Iraq," McGinnis said. But over time, Wellstone became far more deliberate when considering foreign policy decisions and began consulting with the wide range of experts available to him. "When he came to what was he going to do about the Serbs in Kosovo, for example, by that point he was talking to the CIA, the State Department, and other experts, thinking through the different implications of each option," McGinnis said. "He talked to a lot of people, a lot of really smart people."[8]

Wellstone's success was due, in part, to his ability to abide by a set of four principles about how to accomplish his goal of delivering results without compromising principles.

1. *Personalize the issues.* Wellstone understood the power of narrative and was adept at using real-life stories to inform his political platform. In some cases, that meant using his personal experiences (e.g., understanding his brother's mental illness, working with welfare mothers, and taking care of his parents at the end of their lives) as a way to frame an issue. In other cases, it meant using the experience of others (e.g., veterans, victims of domestic violence, and family farmers) to demonstrate his understanding of the circumstances of his constituents' lives.

2. *Be relentless.* The tenaciousness that Wellstone displayed on the Senate floor sometimes grated on his colleagues, but it often produced results. His major victories in the Senate—the gift ban, sex trafficking, job training reform, veterans' health care, and others—all resulted from his willingness to persevere against unlikely odds. Of course, it was this same drive that propelled him to succeed as a young man and later to win his improbable Senate victory in 1990.

3. *Look for unlikely allies.* Critics often pointed to Wellstone's unrepentant liberalism as evidence that he let ideology stand in the way of getting things done. But Wellstone was always more of a populist than an ideologue. When he found opportunities to work with Republicans and conservative Democrats on issues that fit his populist agenda, he took advantage. His alliances with Domenici and other

unlikely allies produced some of his most lasting accomplishments as a senator.

4. *Advocate for those who do not have advocates.* Wellstone knew what it was like to be an outsider, and he was determined to give the various types of advocates and organizers the kind of access to Congress that he never had himself. That meant having an aggressive constituent outreach organization back in Minnesota that worked with underrepresented communities. He was such a constant presence in those communities that he was typically told by their leaders, "You're one of us." And indeed he was—Wellstone felt most at home with people who lacked political clout and representation in Washington.

Wellstone used various methods to put his principles of effective legislating into action, but one of his trademark techniques was to apply a community organizing approach to political advocacy. He believed that grassroots organizing, applied to electoral and legislative politics, was the most effective tool for progressives to contest for power at all levels. While this hardly seems like a radical idea, it represents a significant departure from the conventional wisdom of political strategists and community organizers. Political strategists often eschew grassroots organizing and focus instead on message and media tactics, while community activists frequently dismiss electoral and legislative politics as an ineffective way to a build broad-based social movement. Wellstone was unique in that he pursued both goals: he relied on the power of grassroots organizing to win elections and advocate for a legislative agenda, and he used his position as a political leader to encourage the growth of a broad and diverse movement. "There are," Wellstone said frequently, "three critical ingredients to democratic renewal and progressive change in America: good public policy, grassroots organizing, and electoral politics."

Wellstone heavily emphasized grassroots organizing not only in his political campaigns but also in his legislative work. He maintained deep ties to his political base in Minnesota and engaged them in his work in Washington. He regularly brought people from Minnesota and elsewhere to Washington to testify before Senate committees or to personally lobby senators, and he organized what he called "Accountability Days," when busloads of citizens would come to Washington to hold senators accountable. "This," Wellstone said, "is the essence of participatory democracy."

After Wellstone's death, two senators recalled examples of this technique. "Senator Wellstone chaired a hearing in the Labor Committee on an issue of great concern to American workers," Senator Ted Kennedy said. "A group of low-wage men and women were so excited by the prospect of the hearing that they took a day off from work, boarded buses, and headed for the hearing. When they arrived, they found the room full and the door barred. But Senator Wellstone heard about the workers who were waiting in the hallway, unable to get in. He invited them in and seated them on the dais among the senators attending the hearing."[9]

But it was not enough for Wellstone to simply make Congress more accessible to his constituents; he was interested in delivering results for those constituents. In a floor tribute to Wellstone, Senator Byron Dorgan of North Dakota recalled a story that captured the essence of Wellstone's style of leadership:

> In the last couple months, Paul came up to me while we were in the well of the Senate, and he said: "I was cam-

paigning in Minnesota and I went to an independent auto repair shop, and the major automobile manufacturers would not give the computer codes to these independent auto repair shops. These small independents are telling me that they cannot work on the new cars. They do not have the computer cards for the carburetors, and all those things they have to have to work on these cars. . . . That is unfair, and it is going to drive those folks out of business. This is going to kill the little guy."

He asked if I would hold a hearing on this in my Consumer Subcommittee. I said of course I will. We put together some information on it. The day of the hearing came and Senator Wellstone was to be the lead-off witness. That was not enough for Senator Wellstone. As was his want, in the way he did politics, the hearing room was packed. It was full of mechanics and independent repair shop owners from all across this country. I guess that hearing room holds probably 100 people, and there were 150 people there. Paul had brought his people, the independent repair shop folks, to that hearing as a demonstration of this problem, to say that this problem ought to be fixed.

Paul was the lead-off witness and as was typical with him, with great passion he made the case about the unfairness to the little guy, about the independent repair shops trying to make a living, and how what is happening is unfair to them.

About three weeks ago, right before we completed our work and left for the election, Paul came up to me on the floor of the Senate during a vote. He was holding a sheet of paper. He was flashing this paper and saying, "We won!" His point was that the automobile manufacturers had reached an agreement with the independent repair shops, and that problem had gotten solved.

For Paul, it was about the little guy versus the big guy, about those who did not have the power and those who did.[10]

Although Wellstone's commitment to solving problems is often overlooked by political observers, it was no less real. His principles worked: during his second term, when *Congressional Quarterly* ranked the 535 members of Congress in terms of their effectiveness, he made the top 50.

Sheila's Ascent

As Wellstone settled in as a legislator, Sheila was coming into her own as an advocate and public speaker. It was a transformation that was every bit as dramatic as her husband's maturation as a senator. When Paul won election to the Senate in 1990, Sheila had spent most of her lifetime supporting her husband and caring for their three children, David, Marcia, and Mark. She worked part-time as an aide at the Northfield High School library. She was shy, unassuming, and nervous as a public speaker. Yet she had always had a profound influence on her husband and served as a key behind-the-scenes adviser throughout his career. She had encouraged him to run for auditor in 1982, and she played a pivotal role in the 1990 Senate campaign. "Paul rarely made a decision that Sheila wasn't consulted on or behind," said her longtime friend Dianne Stimson.[11]

After Paul's election, Sheila began playing a more public role in politics and public policy. Early in the first term, she took notice of an alarming state and national crisis. Each year, approximately 1.5 million women were victims of domestic violence. As someone who spent much of her life dedicated to providing a safe and loving home for her family, she was outraged and determined to educate herself on this issue. For a year, she read and listened to people's stories. At shelters in Minnesota and in Washington, she listened to victims of domestic violence recount in horrifying detail the abuse they had suffered. Women sat in circles in shelter living rooms across the state and told her stories so private that they had sometimes never told them before. She listened, learned, and began crafting policy responses to the problem. By the middle of Paul's first term, she was serving as an unpaid member of his legislative staff in Washington.

Over the course of Wellstone's tenure in office, Sheila established herself as one of the nation's leading experts on the problem of domestic violence. Working with her husband, she played a key role in the drafting and passage of the Violence Against Women Act. She had an instrumental role in crafting and passing other pieces of legislation aimed at protecting women and children from the ravages of domestic violence. She was actively involved in raising awareness of international human rights abuses, including the issue of sex trafficking of young women and girls.

Wellstone's Senate colleagues praised Sheila for her unique and influential work in raising their awareness of domestic violence issues. In addition to serving on many national and Minnesota advisory committees in this issue area, she was also appointed by the U.S. Department of Justice and the U.S. Department of Health and Human Services to the Violence Against Women Advisory Council in 1995.

In addition to her domestic violence work, Sheila played an increasingly visible role in Paul's campaigns. She was a shrewd observer of politics and a valuable asset on the campaign trail. Despite her dislike of public speaking, she became a polished and persuasive public speaker. By the end of Paul's second term, political observers in Minnesota began speculating that Sheila would be a formidable political candidate herself.

Going National

As Wellstone's stature as a senator grew, so did his interest in taking on a higher national profile. By the beginning of 1998, he began seriously considering something that he had privately discussed with aides for several years. "Let's win this first," he said privately in 1996 as his reelection campaign drew to a close, "and then we need to start thinking about doing a presidential race." He was eager to emerge not only as a leader on issues like government reform and health care but also as a key player in Democratic politics. He had watched, with growing disappointment, as President Clinton capitulated to Republicans as Clinton's reelection drew closer. He was dismayed by the Democrats' support for the welfare reform bill that passed Congress in the fall of 1996 and believed that his party had retreated from its commitment to the poor.

During the welfare reform debate, which took place in the final months of his reelection campaign, Wellstone argued that supporters of the bill did not understand the severity of poverty in America and that the plight of the nation's poor was far worse—and more complex—than most Americans realized. As one of the few members of the Senate who had actually worked closely with welfare recipients, he was incensed at what he saw as the scapegoating of the poor. He vowed to raise awareness of the plight of the poor in America by taking a poverty tour of the country. He promised to visit both urban and rural areas and to raise the country's awareness of the persistent problem of poverty in the country. It was an idea borrowed from Robert Kennedy, whose tour in the 1960s of poor areas in the South gave poverty a public face.

The idea of a poverty tour had been met with derision

by Wellstone's opponents and was opposed by many of his own aides, who worried about the political consequences of seeming more concerned with the nation's poor than with his middle-class constituents in Minnesota. But the issue had little impact on the campaign, and after Wellstone was reelected he delivered on his promise. In the summer of 1997, he began what would be a seven-month tour of the nation's most impoverished communities. He traveled to Mississippi, Louisiana, Chicago, Los Angeles, and Harlan County in Kentucky, where Sheila's grandparents had lived. The tour was a success. A group of cameras accompanied him to his stops, and Wellstone received considerable, mostly positive, attention from the national media.

His travels convinced Wellstone that he could play an important role in the 2000 presidential election, and he became increasingly interested in making a run. Wellstone wanted to run for president because he saw it as an extraordinary organizing opportunity. In an unpublished draft of *The Conscience of a Liberal*, he describes in detail several successful local organizing initiatives, but then adds:

> The only cautionary note I would sound about the organizing I've observed throughout the country is the danger of "dead-end localism". It makes sense that the victories are won by people where they live. The big victories are those won by people themselves—that is empowerment—and ordinary citizens make a difference in a local context. They don't fly around the world in a jet.
>
> But if the victories, no matter how dramatic and important, never affect national or international centers of decision-making power, which can crucially define the quality, or lack of quality of the lives of people, then we are still not seriously contesting for power.

This is the central challenge for progressive politics: How to build the local victories into a strong national and international presence. Right now the whole does not equal the sum of the parts. As a United States Senator, I am excited by all the good work. I love to recount these local organizing victories, all of the amazing people I've met who have done so much to make their communities better. But I am also painfully aware of how little power progressives have at the national level. The goal is how to make local grassroots organizing, where citizens make a real difference, a key factor in determining the future of national politics.[12]

This idea was a critical component of Wellstone's political philosophy. It was not sufficient to win small, local victories. Contesting for power meant going national.

On April 8, 1998, Wellstone became the first candidate to declare his presidential ambitions when he formally announced the creation of a presidential exploratory committee, a move that allowed him to raise money to pay for travel and campaign staff. Although he did not expect to get the Democratic nomination, much less wind up residing at 1600 Pennsylvania Avenue, he understood the symbolic power of a presidential campaign. Running for president, Wellstone said, would allow him to take advantage of his unique ability to organize, galvanize, and build support for an "energized, effective citizen politics."

At his campaign stops, Wellstone was unambiguous about his desire to go through with the campaign. He visited Iowa and New Hampshire several times and spoke at local Democratic Party gatherings. Democratic activists in both states received him warmly. In his speeches, he delivered a message focused on reform and economic opportunity. The question Democrats should be asking in the campaign,

Wellstone said, is "Why is the United States, at the peak of its economic performance, still being told we can't provide a good education for each child, health care for every family and a living wage for every worker?" It was a message that liberal Democrats—which constitute a large majority of the party's primary voters and caucus goers—had not heard from a presidential candidate in years. It was during one of his many trips to Iowa that Wellstone stumbled onto what would become his trademark line. He tells the story in an unpublished manuscript draft:

> I was speaking to 300 Johnson County Democrats when Tom Vilsak, one of the Democratic candidates for Governor (he went on to win big upset primary and general election victories) kiddingly yelled out, "Paul, why are you coming to Iowa all the time?"
>
> I responded, "I come to Iowa to represent the Democratic wing of the Democratic Party."
>
> The place went nuts. I knew this was a winner. That these Democrats knew exactly what I meant and many were in agreement! In New Hampshire when I spoke to Central Committee Democrats (these were the party regulars), I said the same thing—and there was the same reaction. Even Al Gore supporters . . . were laughing when they knew they shouldn't.[13]

From that point on, Wellstone repeatedly used that line to describe his politics. By December, the decision seemed to have already been made. "Things really crystallized for me in Iowa," he told a reporter at the time. "I got up early and said, 'This is inside me because I want to drive big money out of politics and drive people in.'"[14]

But the campaign was not to be. As he deliberated his

decision back home in Minnesota, Wellstone went to the Mayo Clinic for a routine checkup of his chronic back pain that had been plaguing him for years. Doctors told him that the condition of his back had worsened and that a presidential campaign, with its demanding schedule and hours of traveling in small planes and in automobiles, could seriously damage his long-term health. In early January 1999, he announced that he would not run for the presidency. Wellstone's disappointment was clear. He badly wanted to run and told associates that he knew how difficult it would be to stand on the sidelines as other candidates got into the race. "I apologize for all the cabinet positions I promised," he joked.[15]

Living in Pain

If Wellstone felt frustrated by his inability to take on the rigors of a presidential campaign, he was also discouraged by the fact that his chronic back injury had still not been diagnosed. Throughout much of his adult life, he was in constant and often excruciating back pain. An accomplished long-distance runner, he was forced early in his first term to give up running and was confined to working out on the Stairmaster in his condominiums in St. Paul and Washington. He walked with a marked limp, wearing down the toe of his right shoe because it dragged behind him when he walked. On long car drives, he was forced to recline the passenger seat and lie down on his stomach. On his biweekly flights from Minnesota to Washington, he stood whenever possible because of his back pain and used the opportunity to introduce himself to all the passengers on the plane.

Doctors did not definitively know what was causing the pain. Wellstone blamed it on an old wrestling injury, and various doctors diagnosed it as sciatica or vertebrae injury.

After his visit to the Mayo Clinic, Wellstone finally decided to have surgery even though it was against his own long-standing wishes. The surgery failed to solve the problem, adding to his frustration and general mistrust of doctors. Three years later, he would be diagnosed as having a mild form of multiple sclerosis.

Despite being in constant pain, Wellstone rarely took any form of medication to treat it, and he maintained an almost fanatical workout schedule. He insisted that his staff incorporate time in his schedule for his daily workout, which consisted of weight training and a sixty-minute Stairmaster workout on the most difficult setting. He exercised six days a week and claimed that the last time he went two days in a row without working out was when he was in high school. He was proud of his commitment to his physical health and relished the fact that he was in better shape than most people half his age.

When Wellstone first arrived in the Senate, he refused to use the gym and workout facilities reserved for senators and instead asked the capitol police if he could use their facilities. They skeptically agreed, and Wellstone became a daily fixture in the police gym. When the officers held their annual pull-up competition, Wellstone entered and bragged that he would win. Despite their doubts, he made good on his prediction and won the competition. He once joked that it was his proudest accomplishment in the Senate.

A Surrogate for Bradley

After Wellstone dropped out of the presidential race, he quickly endorsed a colleague who shared his passion for athletics—former senator and NBA basketball star Bill Bradley. Wellstone immediately immersed himself in Bradley's campaign. Throughout the summer and into the fall, he traveled across the country on Bradley's behalf, dedicating at least three days a month to the campaign. By the end of the year, he had become Bradley's leading surrogate, and he and Sheila had formed a deep personal friendship with Bradley and his wife, Josephine. In his speeches and campaign appearances, Wellstone's dedication to Bradley was evident. He spoke passionately about Bradley's commitment to ending poverty and to addressing the deteriorating race relations.

But campaigning for Bradley was bittersweet. As usual, Wellstone loved being on the campaign trail and firing up enthusiastic crowds. As one newspaper columnist put it after seeing him speak, "Wellstone in front of a crowd is plainly a man who enjoys his work."[16] But privately, the overwhelmingly positive response he received on the campaign trail made Wellstone think of the campaign that might have been. His fire-and-brimstone speeches often overshadowed Bradley's and left some members of the audience wondering aloud if they would have supported a Wellstone candidacy. A typical response came from one Bradley supporter after seeing Wellstone speak at a January rally in New Hampshire: "If he were running for president this year, no question—I'd be with him."[17] Another supporter told him excitedly, "You must melt the snow in Minnesota every time you talk!"[18] Wellstone wondered aloud to friends and aides about the impact his candidacy would have had on the race.

After Bradley suffered decisive defeats in Iowa and New Hampshire, he withdrew from the race in March 2000. Although Wellstone quickly endorsed Al Gore for president, he spent little time campaigning for him. Instead, he returned his focus to a full agenda in Washington and to the increasingly pressing question of what he was going to do with his political future.

Breaking a Promise

When Wellstone announced in 1990 that he would only seek two terms, twelve years in the U.S. Senate seemed like an eternity. "I want to give this all that I have," he said at his first press conference as senator-elect. "I'm tired of grading papers and I wanted to get out of it, but eventually I'll go back to teaching."[19] But by the middle of his second term in office, Wellstone's reality had changed profoundly. He had grown into the job of senator and had learned how to use his leverage to get things done. "I just don't see how I can walk away from this," he often said in private as his second term drew to a close. But breaking his promise was a big political risk. Whether or not they agreed with him on all issues, Minnesotans believed he was a person of integrity who kept his word. The broken pledge had the potential to undermine the foundation on which Wellstone's reputation had been built.

But running for a third Senate term was not Wellstone's only option for staying in public office. As his second term drew to a close, he grew increasingly interested in running for governor. While he enjoyed being a legislator, serving as Minnesota's chief executive would give him far-ranging influence over the state's budget priorities. As governor, he could have a more direct impact on issues like health care and education than he could as senator.

And a run for governor would give Wellstone a chance to unseat Jesse Ventura, the former professional wrestler who stunned political observers by winning a three-way election in 1998. Despite their surface similarities—both were former wrestlers known for their from-the-hip straightforwardness and willingness to buck convention—Wellstone and Ventura disliked one another. Wellstone blanched at what he perceived to be Ventura's bashing of public service and his "buddy, you're on your own" political philosophy. Ventura viewed Wellstone as an out-of-touch ideologue. "We have very different views of public service," Wellstone said publicly. In private he said Ventura was a charlatan who used his populist persona to self-satisfying aims. The difference between the two, Wellstone said, was like the difference between "real wrestling and fake wrestling."

But a race between Ventura and Wellstone would not materialize. Despite his dislike for the governor—and a firm conviction that he would defeat Ventura if he ran against him—by the fall of 2000 Wellstone was leaning against a run. He had listened to friends and advisors tell him that the job of governor was not one for which he was well suited. As the chief executive of the state, he would be forced to deal with issues that held little interest for him—particularly the intricacies of the state budgeting process. In the Senate, he was free to do the advocating and legislating that fit his personal style.

After the extraordinary elections of 2000, Wellstone made his decision final. With the presidential election between Al Gore and George W. Bush being decided by the Supreme Court and the balance of power in the Senate being equally shared—there was now an even fifty-fifty split of Democrats and Republicans—he said he could not walk away from the fight in Washington. In January 2001, he sat with Sheila in front of a crowded room of reporters in a neighborhood St. Paul restaurant and announced his intention to seek a third term to the Senate. He spoke for several minutes and ended by saying, "I feel great about the chemistry I have with Minnesotans, and . . . I will give this campaign my all."

6

Last Campaign

Surely, politics is made with the head,
but it is certainly not made with the
head alone.

WELLSTONE'S LAST CAMPAIGN would be
his most difficult. Although he enjoyed the highest approval
ratings of his career, polls showed that a clear majority was
opposed to his decision to seek a third term. "He said he'd
run for two terms and then out," one poll respondent told a
reporter. "He should stay by that. That's pretty plain and
simple."[1] A promise was a promise; Wellstone's integrity,
which in the past had served as a buffer to charges of being
too liberal, was suddenly in question. Republicans leaped at
the chance to portray him as an out-of-touch career politician. "[He] went to Washington as Professor Wellstone and
he's now morphed into Potomac Paul," said one.[2] He was
vulnerable: in addition to breaking his promise, Wellstone
would once again be the target of an intensive and costly

Republican campaign. But this time, instead of facing a weak candidate like Rudy Boschwitz, he would run against the hand-picked candidate of the White House.

In the months following Wellstone's announcement, the Republicans' search for his opponent unfolded like a dramatic soap opera. Initially, a group of influential Minnesota Republicans urged a state representative named Tim Pawlenty to seek the party's nomination. But the White House had other ideas. During the 2000 presidential campaign, St. Paul mayor Norm Coleman had caught the attention of George W. Bush's chief political strategist, Karl Rove. As one of Bush's earliest supporters in Minnesota, Coleman had visited regularly with Bush and Rove during the campaign and had impressed Rove as a capable and loyal political centrist—the kind of ally the White House needed in Washington.

In early April 2001, while in Washington for a conference of mayors, Coleman had the opportunity to meet privately with Bush. At that meeting, and during a subsequent trip to the White House a week later, Bush, Rove, and other senior administration officials urged Coleman to drop his intended bid for governor and run for Senate instead. In the spring of 2001, he surprised state Republican leaders by announcing that he intended to take on Wellstone.

The announcement complicated Pawlenty's plans. The majority leader of the House, he had spent the previous year deciding between running for governor or for senator. At first, he wanted to run for governor, but the group of influential party insiders scuttled those plans by publicly urging him to forgo a governor's race. Pawlenty was persuaded, and by the time Norm Coleman made clear his interest in running against Wellstone, he had already made up his mind.

He scheduled a news conference for April 18 to announce his intention to run for Senate. The night before, he received a call at home from Karl Rove, who urged him not to challenge Coleman for the Senate nomination but to run for governor instead. Pawlenty listened to Rove but told him he was sticking to his plans.

The following day, the White House increased the pressure. That morning, Pawlenty was driving his kids to school when his cellular phone rang. It was Vice President Dick Cheney on the other line. Cheney told Pawlenty that he was calling on behalf of the White House to ask him to "stand down" and forgo a run for the Senate. The call came ninety minutes before Pawlenty's news conference, and it worked. Pawlenty agreed to Cheney's request and in a dramatic appearance before a packed room of reporters announced that he would not run for Senate. "On behalf of the president and the vice president of the United States, [Cheney] asked that I not go forward. . . . For the good of the party, for the good of the effort [against Wellstone] I agreed not to pursue an exploratory campaign," he said.[3]

It was an extraordinary intervention by the White House into state politics. The episode stunned political observers in Minnesota and propelled Norm Coleman to the status of presumed Republican nominee. From Washington, Wellstone watched the drama unfold with a sense of bemusement. "What in the world have I done to attract all of this attention and be such a big target? . . . I have a big twinkle in my eye about all this," he said when asked about Cheney's intervention.[4] Although he knew Coleman would be a strong candidate, Wellstone looked forward to the opportunity to turn the Senate election into a referendum on Bush. The campaign was on.

A New Opponent

Norm Coleman was a onetime Democrat whom one journalist described as "a clean-cut pin-striped cigar-smoking law-and-order prosecutor who liked schmoozing with business leaders a whole lot better than with welfare rights activists."[5] His career was defined by a love of deal making and a willingness to reinvent himself according to political expediency. Although he endorsed Wellstone for Senate in 1996, the following year Coleman switched parties and ran for governor as a Republican. He easily secured his party's nomination before losing to Jesse Ventura in the general election.

Despite the 1998 loss, Coleman was viewed as one of the Republican Party's brightest lights in Minnesota. As mayor of St. Paul, he led an impressive revitalization of the city's downtown and brokered a string of high-profile business deals, including a deal that brought professional hockey back to Minnesota. His success, he said, resulted from his determination to put aside political differences to get things done. "I will reach across party lines, cast aside the partisan bickering and posturing and will work with the president to get things done," he said when announcing his candidacy. "I am a prophet of hope."[6]

For the next year and a half, Wellstone and Coleman engaged in a campaign that was largely defined by the issue of corporate accountability. When news broke in late 2001 that the corporate giant Enron was collapsing due to mismanagement, press accounts described President Bush's close association with Enron's top executives. The scandal presented Wellstone with an opportunity to put Coleman on the defensive. He criticized Coleman's close association with the White House and his ties to corporate interests. By the summer of 2002, Democrats had gained traction on the issue: several national polls showed that Americans were increasingly skeptical of Republicans' ability to effectively handle the accounting scandals. The issue clearly concerned Coleman, who was, in the words of one reporter, "confronted by an incumbent who is fast making corporate accountability a front-and-center issue."[7] In late August, Coleman announced his support for tougher sanctions against "corporate evildoers" and filmed a campaign ad addressing the corporate scandals.[8] Going into the month of September, the Wellstone campaign sensed that momentum was on its side. That would change almost overnight.

A Turning Point

As the campaign entered the month of September, Republicans took the offensive, both domestically and internationally. The Bush administration intensified its calls for regime change in Iraq after being criticized for failing to engage the public and international leaders in a discussion of Saddam Hussein's threat. With the first anniversary of the September 11 terrorist attacks approaching, the White House hoped to transform the political debate into a discussion about the potential for war. By the middle of September, they had succeeded: the war in Iraq had eclipsed other issues in the campaign. Buoyed by a resurgence of Bush's popularity in the wake of the September 11 anniversary, Norm Coleman ripped Wellstone for opposing the president's Iraq policy and for being soft on the war on terror. Having already said during the summer that the United States in Afghanistan "would have lost more lives on the ground if we followed [Wellstone's] judgment," his campaign now charged that Wellstone was "among the worst enemies of America's defense."[9]

The attacks began taking a toll. In September, for the first time in the campaign, Wellstone's internal polls showed him trailing Coleman. And he would soon have to take a politically risky vote in the Senate. Congress was scheduled to consider in early October a resolution authorizing military action in Iraq. Wellstone would be forced to go on record on an increasingly popular White House policy. For weeks, he had argued that he would only support such a resolution if the United States received United Nations' authorization and had criticized as "too openended" a draft resolution that gave Bush authority to attack Iraq without the support of the international community. As the vote on the resolution approached, every Democratic candidate in the half dozen closest races for Senate announced his support for the measure, and political observers speculated that Wellstone's career was in peril. One top Democratic strategist was so convinced that the vote would cost Wellstone the election that he wrote Wellstone's campaign manager an angry e-mail: "It makes me almost physically ill to even contemplate spending [money] on a candidate who decides to commit suicide—however principled and otherwise defensible."[10]

Despite the political pressure, Wellstone never seriously considered voting for a resolution that gave the United States authorization to take unilateral military action against Iraq. In early October, he acknowledged that the resolution was widely popular in the Senate and that opposing it could cost him the campaign, but he said he would vote against it. "Acting on our own might be a sign of our power," he said. "[But] acting sensibly, in concert with our allies and with bipartisan congressional support, would be a sign of our strength."[11] In the end, he said, the issue was about whether he felt justified in putting American lives at risk in Iraq. "We're talking about a lot of sons and daughters, a lot of Minnesota sons and daughters that could be in harm's way. And I think it's extremely important for the United States to do this the right way, and not the wrong way."[12]

Wellstone knew the potential consequences of his decision and acknowledged that he would have preferred to be dealing with other issues. "With five weeks to go, at the end of 12 [years] in the Senate, of course I wonder what the effect will be," he told a reporter. "To me, this is the personally and intellectually honest decision, and that's the one I should make. And I don't really think I have any other choice but to make it, because how could you do otherwise? It's a life-and-death question. . . . I'm not making any decision that I don't believe in."[13] When asked how he felt after making his announcement, he said simply, "My soul is resting."[14]

But if Wellstone was taking a political risk, he was also convinced that support among Minnesotans for unilateral action in Iraq was soft. He was optimistic that even those who disagreed with his position would respect him for standing up for what he felt was right. "I know the conventional wisdom among Republicans is that this is the issue that will do him in," Wellstone said, speaking of himself. "But I think people want you to do what you think is right. I think people want to support the president, but they're very worried about doing it alone. . . . I think people in Minnesota have the same concerns that I have."[15]

Wellstone's internal campaign polling suggested that he was right. Braced for the possibility that his support was continuing to erode, his campaign polled Minnesotans immediately following his announcement. The results were remarkable. Though Wellstone had been trailing Coleman in late September, the data showed that Wellstone's approval rating was going *up* and that he had surged ahead of Coleman by five points. In a three-week period—a time when many observers thought he had effectively lost the election—Wellstone went from a four-point deficit to a five-point lead. Other polls confirmed these results: five separate polls taken in late October, including those of the state's two major newspapers, showed Wellstone holding a lead of between three and eight percentage points. One of those polls, taken by the *Star Tribune*, showed that Minnesotans were evenly divided on the question of who would best handle the Iraq situation and that Wellstone was the strong choice of people identifying the economy or the looming war as the most important problem facing the country.

Wellstone's handling of the war in Iraq stood in stark contrast to his handling of the first Gulf War. Although he voted in both cases against using military force against Saddam Hussein, Wellstone was marginalized in 1991 by his own insolence and indignation. In addition to taking an unpopular vote, he also offended key constituent groups as well as his colleagues and the president. His approval ratings plummeted to below 30 percent. Nearly twelve years later, he voted against a popular war in the midst of a bruising reelection campaign, and he moved into the lead against his opponent. By then, Wellstone had demonstrated to his colleagues and his constituents that he belonged in the U.S. Senate, regardless of whether he took unpopular votes. In 1991, veterans' groups protested angrily when he staged a press conference at the Vietnam Wall; by 2002, veterans rushed to his defense after his vote against the war, and he received a political lift instead of a setback.

The Final Week

By the end of October, Wellstone was confident of victory but running like an underdog. He insisted on maintaining a grueling schedule, crossing the state in his green bus or by prop plane. As the campaign entered the final stages, the intensity increased. President Bush made his third campaign trip in support of Coleman, and media attention focused on a series of debates between the candidates. As the stress of the campaign mounted, Wellstone relied on Sheila's reassuring presence to stay focused. He asked her to join him for all campaign events, even though his usual practice was to avoid having her travel with him by plane, out of fear that they would both go down in an accident. When his daughter, Marcia, who had taken a leave from her job as a high school teacher to work on the campaign for the fall, asked to join them for the final days, he acceded.

Wellstone began the last weekend of October at a frenetic pace. A debate with Coleman was planned for the night of Sunday, October 26, in Duluth, giving Wellstone an opportunity to spend the previous day campaigning on the Iron Range, firing up supporters at "get out the vote" rallies. The trip coincided with another event in the region that Wellstone wanted to attend: the funeral of the father of one of Wellstone's most faithful supporters, a state representative named Tom Rukavina. The plan was for Wellstone to fly up to the Iron Range town of Eveleth to attend the funeral in nearby Virginia, Minnesota, and then to spend the rest of the day campaigning on the Iron Range. He would be joined by Sheila, Marcia, and three staff members.

The morning of October 25 was cold and rainy. Wellstone's pilot, nervous about the conditions, made repeated

inquiries into the weather in Eveleth. After initially deciding to cancel the trip due to the potential for freezing rain
and poor visibility, the pilot changed his mind when reports
came in that the conditions were improving. The Wellstones were picked up at their condominium in St. Paul and
driven to Holman Field, the downtown St. Paul airport,
where they got an update on the weather from the pilot.
Wellstone, who was a nervous flier, sat impatiently in the
lobby and asked the pilot to double-check the weather.
Moments later, a charter plane, which had come in from
Duluth, landed at the airport. The pilot of that plane, upon
hearing of Wellstone's nervousness, assured him that he had
run into no problems. The weather, he said, was not ideal
but certainly acceptable for flying. At approximately 9:30
a.m., the plane took off from Holman Field. It made it to
within two miles of the Eveleth airport before crashing in a
boggy forest.

Last Days
and Legacy

> Certainly all historical experience
> confirms the truth—that man would not
> have attained the possible unless time
> and again he had reached out for the
> impossible.

WELLSTONE WAS KILLED just twelve days
before Election Day. An investigation by the National
Transportation and Safety Board would later conclude that
the cause of the crash was pilot error, not bad weather. In
the surreal aftermath of Wellstone's death, his campaign
advisers had little time to absorb the depth of the loss.
Instead, they and Wellstone's surviving sons focused on
finding a candidate to replace him on the ballot and quickly
came up with their choice: Walter Mondale. At seventy-
one, Mondale was Minnesota's elder statesman—a former
senator, vice president, and ambassador. On the morning of
October 27, campaign manager Jeff Blodgett, David Well-

stone, and friend David Lillehaug visited Mondale at his law office. In an emotional meeting, David Wellstone asked Mondale to step in on his father's behalf. Mondale told the group that he would likely run but would not announce his intentions publicly until after Wellstone's public memorial service, planned for the following Tuesday. As word spread of a possible Mondale candidacy, many observers speculated that Coleman stood little chance of winning. Polls taken at the time showed Mondale holding a lead against Norm Coleman.

The memorial service was held at Williams Arena, home of the University of Minnesota's basketball team. Twenty thousand people attended the service, and thousands more watched it live on television. Also attending the service were dozens of former and current elected officials, including former president Bill Clinton, Senate Majority Leader Trent Lott, and Minnesota governor Jesse Ventura.

For four hours, eulogizers paid tribute to their loved ones. The three staff members were remembered first. Will McLaughlin's older brother talked about how Will thought of Wellstone as a surrogate for their deceased father. A friend of Tom Lapic described him as a "wise and comforting presence" and a trustworthy friend. Mary McEvoy was honored by the president of the University of Minnesota, where she was a professor, as one of the university's "brightest lights." Following the eulogies for the staffers, the Wellstones were remembered. Marcia Wellstone Markuson's best friend described her "contagious smile" and effusive charm. Sheila Wellstone was memorialized as an exceptional wife and mother who touched many lives and "made us all bigger than we were."

Wellstone was eulogized last. Four speakers—Wellstone's two sons, his former student and friend Rick Kahn, and his

friend Senator Tom Harkin—spoke of his life and impact.
Dave Wellstone talked about his father's deep commitment
to teaching and athletics and his parents' easy relationship.
Mark Wellstone said that his favorite memory of his father
was having him as a wrestling coach in junior high school.
He went on to talk about what his mother meant to him and
to his father: "Everything." Harkin paid tribute to "my best
friend." His voice cracking, he recalled Wellstone's sharp
wit and commitment to ordinary people, describing him as a
leader with "a spine of steel." Recalling Wellstone's insis-
tence that people refer to him by his first name, Harkin said,
"No one ever wore the title of Senator better and used it
less."

But Rick Kahn delivered a speech that overshadowed the
other eulogies. For all of his adult life, Kahn had been one of
Wellstone's closest friends. He met Wellstone as a first-year
student at Carleton and quickly became a key part of Wellstone's organizing efforts. After graduating, Kahn deepened
his friendship with Wellstone, assisting in his political
activism and later serving as the volunteer treasurer for each
of Wellstone's campaigns. As a quiet and soft-spoken man,
Kahn's personality contrasted sharply with Wellstone's. But
his former professor was also Kahn's hero, and it was manifest by his fierce loyalty and reluctance to criticize Wellstone's judgment. "Everyone should be as blessed to have a
friend like you," Wellstone wrote to Kahn in the dedication
of his autobiography.

But when Rick Kahn stood up to deliver his eulogy, those
who knew him witnessed a stunning transformation. He
began by describing Wellstone's fiery first speech to DFL
Party delegates in 1982. Within moments, Kahn himself
was on fire. He used the eulogy to exhort Wellstone's supporters to carry on the campaign. "A week from today, Paul

Wellstone's name will not be on the ballot," Kahn said. "But there will be a choice just the same. . . . either keep his legacy alive, or bring it forever to an end!" In an instant, the memorial service turned into a political rally. Kahn spoke for twenty-five minutes, concluding his remarks with an odd request for Republicans to concede the election out of respect to his legacy. In the devastating wake of Wellstone death, emotions had overcome Wellstone's friend; the eulogy went too far. The speech was heartfelt but utterly self-defeating. In his attempt to honor Wellstone's memory, Kahn inadvertently made the subject of the memorial service not the Wellstones but Kahn himself.

The memorial service was a disaster. Viewers were outraged, Wellstone's supporters were embarrassed, and Governor Jesse Ventura walked out of the ceremony, complaining that Democrats had used the gathered mourners as political props. The tone of the campaign immediately changed. The galvanized Republican opposition, which had suspended its campaign after Wellstone died, resumed its campaign with vigor. Republican operatives were ready and willing to pounce on mistakes in the memorial service and even accused Democrats (falsely, it was later revealed) of scripting the audience to boo when Republicans were shown on the arena's video monitors. Wellstone's supporters had been put on the defensive in an instant.

By the time Walter Mondale entered the race the following day, anger about the memorial service had become the central issue in the campaign. Mondale was unable to regain the momentum that had been lost. The results of the election were announced in the early morning hours of November 6, thirteen days after Wellstone died. Mondale lost to Coleman by two percentage points, a difference of less than fifty thousand votes out of 2.2 million cast.

Coda

Donald Mathews, the North Carolina political science professor whose book had played such an instructive role in Wellstone's life, was recently asked if he remembered Wellstone as a student. Mathews, who is in poor health and has difficulty speaking, replied simply, "Who could forget Paul?"[1]

Indeed, few Minnesotans have. For more than a year after his death, green Wellstone lawn signs still sat in front yards across Minnesota. Schools, buildings, and parks have been renamed for Wellstone. Biographies, a documentary film, and scores of articles about Wellstone's life and legacy have been written or are currently in production. A nonprofit organization, Wellstone Action, was established to carry on Wellstone's work by training progressive activists nationwide—in less than two years, the organization added ninety thousand members and trained nearly ten thousand activists. Liberal activists are engaged in a lively discussion of ways to continue pushing Wellstone's work forward without him, and some of his supporters even sport bumper stickers and buttons posing the evangelizing question, "What Would Wellstone Do?" At the same time, some of Wellstone's more unforgiving critics have responded to the outpouring with a bumper sticker of their own: "He's dead. Get over it."

It is hardly surprising that Wellstone stirred up such passion in both his supporters and his opponents. His willingness to stand up for his beliefs evoked both admiration and disdain. Wellstone accepted that many people would disagree with him—after all, he spent a career teaching his students the importance of using conflict as a tool for achieving social progress. But it wasn't just his liberalism that earned him such deep admiration. He was successful—he spoke his mind, but he also won elections and was an accomplished legislator. Wellstone understood that conflict alone was not enough. As an organizer and as a politician, he learned to use compromise and a sense of humor to get results. In the end, he stood out from other liberal politicians because he was too effective for his critics to dismiss.

From the earliest days of his career, Wellstone began his speeches by saying, "I view this gathering with a sense of history," and he would place his struggle—whatever it was at the time—against the backdrop of a larger historical context. Wellstone undoubtedly wanted to be a part of history when it was written, and although time will judge his legacy and its impact on progressive politics, he will likely be remembered alongside some of the great Midwestern progressives. "I have always thought of Paul Wellstone in relation to the 1920s," said columnist E. J. Dionne. "In the 1920s you had these extraordinary progressives, people like George Norris, Fiorello LaGuardia, and Robert Lafollette, who were fighting very hard, knowing as they were doing it that they were going to lose a lot of fights. Almost all of the ideas that those people fought for in the '20s came to fruition when Roosevelt became president; their ideas became the ideas of the New Deal. I think Wellstone was a figure like those 1920s progressives, who understood that you can hold up a torch and know that someday people would come along and join your torch with a lot of other torches."[2]

One of Wellstone's favorite movies was a little-known 1979 film called *Northern Lights,* the story of a group of Scandinavian farmers in North Dakota in 1915 who organize a revolt to get higher grain prices and protect their way of life from powerful business and government interests.

"Paul loved that movie," said Jeff Blodgett. "I think in some ways he wished he lived in that era."[3] It is not surprising that Wellstone was often compared to the great prairie populists. For nearly two decades, he led protests and direct actions across the Minnesota plains, galvanizing farmers, getting arrested, and becoming a rousing political orator. When he ran for Senate in 1990, he began his stump speech by promising to run "a campaign that will restore people's faith in politics, a campaign that will light a prairie fire that will sweep Rudy Boschwitz and all his money and wealthy benefactors out of Washington like a pack of grasshoppers!"[4] He campaigned from a green bus with a speaker's platform on the back because he wanted to campaign "like Harry Truman."

Wellstone had much in common with the great Midwestern progressive populists. These were leaders with strong convictions and feisty temperaments who wanted to give workers, immigrants, and other disenfranchised citizens a voice in politics. Known as powerful orators, they cared about social and economic justice, higher wages, fair-trade policies, health care, and providing a social safety net for society's most vulnerable. Like these progressive leaders, Wellstone spoke eloquently, stuck to his principles, and fought relentlessly for an ambitious agenda. His foes considered him intransigent and sometimes annoying, but he was deeply admired for his ability to stand up for what he believed in. He also had ambitions for himself, and like many of his predecessors, he ran for president (if only briefly) as part of a broad effort to push forward progressive politics. And like the other great Midwestern progressive populists, Wellstone was an idealist to the core. "Paul did not come out of wealth," Mondale said. "He was not the establishment. He was not running in order to make the comfortable more comfortable. He was running—serving—in order to make life better for people on the edges and that hadn't gotten a break."5

Yet in many ways Wellstone was a new type of progressive leader. Instead of relying solely on an agrarian, trade union base of supporters, he forged impressive coalitions with environmentalists, laborers, immigrants, gays and lesbians, and people of color. He brought these groups together, often literally under one roof, and they all were able to say, "He's one of us." From the perspective of political campaigning, Wellstone was a trailblazer. He was a community organizer in every sense and was able to apply the lessons of grassroots organizing to electoral politics in a way that had not been done before. Wellstone was also unique in that he was a prairie populist who came out of the civil rights movement in the American South. The historian Eric Fure-Slocum, a Wellstone friend, said, "Paul managed to soak up and place himself squarely in the Midwestern farmer-labor tradition, while also bringing to it the inspiration of the Southern Civil Rights movement and the pragmatism of the community organizing tradition."6

Wellstone drew from both the populist and progressive traditions, and he updated and reinvigorated both. He was a fiery speaker and an organizer, just as the old-time Midwestern populists had been. That populist fire gave new life to the traditional liberal agenda. At the same time, as a progressive legislator he was able to broaden the traditional populist economic message to include concerns for issues like social justice, civil rights, and the environment. Unlike traditional populists, Wellstone was an internationalist; where his predecessors focused narrowly on a farmer-labor agenda and were often considered protectionists and even nativists, Wellstone was conversant with and intensely interested in international affairs. He gave populism a broader appeal and greater relevance to the contemporary world. In other words, Wellstone updated for today the old-fashioned, Depression-era populism that he had loved so much and that had been almost forgotten. It is hardly surprising that a Minnesotan would be the person to combine and electrify both traditions. After all, this is the state where the liberal Democratic Party and the populist Farmer-Labor Party had joined forces to create an unbeatable political force sixty years earlier.

As much as Wellstone fit into these traditions, he was clearly his own man, and much of his power came from the force of his personality. "People respond to causes but people also respond to people," said E. J. Dionne. "And there was an irresistible effervescence about Wellstone that I think made people believe in possibilities that they might not have believed in if he hadn't shown up in their living room and said 'yeah, you can do this thing.'"[7] But his success lay not only in his ability to move his constituents; he was also an effective U.S. senator. "Some people would look at Paul and say he was an ideological person, and maybe he was," said Ohio Republican senator Mike DeWine. "But he was also a very practical person and very results oriented. Paul wanted to make a difference in people's lives. . . . To do this in the Senate you have to reach across party lines and get things done. Paul could convert rhetoric into something that was legislative: action that would actually change people's lives."[8]

Although he had an undeniably impressive record of legislative accomplishments for someone who served most of his two terms in the minority, Wellstone's legacy will not be as a legislator. He will, however, be remembered in the U.S. Senate. "There wasn't anybody like Paul," said Senator

Hillary Rodham Clinton. "He was a very important part of the whole Senate atmosphere; he often reminded people what was too easy to forget around here . . . [that] there are millions and millions of people out there who might never even know our names but if we don't stand up for them nobody else will." Clinton's colleague Senator Tim Johnson agreed. "Clearly Paul changed the Senate," Johnson said. "You got what you saw in his case, he didn't bend a bit, he became a real conscience for the Senate. I think that's why he had such a high level of respect even from people on the other side of the aisle who didn't necessarily agree with his views. Paul's personal style was so inclusive that even people who were on the opposite side politically had enormous personal respect and appreciation for him."[9]

In the aftermath of Wellstone's death, many of his supporters have found it difficult to move on. Democrats across the country were roundly defeated in the 2002 congressional elections, and some of the losses were blamed on the controversial memorial service. The service likely cost Walter Mondale the election, and as a result Norm Coleman is a U.S. senator. Despite an impressive performance by Democrats in Minnesota in 2004, George W. Bush's reelection as president was equally disappointing to Wellstone's supporters. If ever there was a time when they wanted to hear one of Wellstone's rowdy speeches, it is now.

But the primary lesson that Wellstone's life held for others is the imperative of finding joy in politics. Wellstone refused to crumble in the face of adversity, and he never drifted in his political views. He simply loved politics. Rare was the occasion when Wellstone was conflicted by indecision, and he delighted in that freedom. As E. J. Dionne recalled, he brimmed with exuberance. "There was always a little kid in Wellstone," Dionne said. "There was this almost naïve energy and you knew it from the way he walked. He didn't just walk. He bounded in. He bounced around."[10] Like his hero Hubert Humphrey, Wellstone embodied the prototypical happy warrior originally described by Wordsworth—someone who is consumed by battles but finds comfort in his own resolve. Armed with a singleness of purpose, Wellstone was, as Wordsworth wrote, as "happy as a lover, and attired with sudden brightness."[11]

Paul Wellstone lived an extraordinary life. As a boy, he went from juvenile delinquent to accomplished athlete and star student. He gained admission to graduate school only after staging a sit-in at the dean's office. At Carleton, he was awarded tenure after his students organized and protested the college's decision to fire him. He came from nowhere to run for Senate and to defeat a popular incumbent. And as a senator, he went from unbending purist to master of the institution. In a life cut short, Wellstone left behind a legacy of persistence, integrity, passion, and, not least, hope. "We must believe that it is the darkness before the dawn of a beautiful new world," wrote Wellstone's favorite writer, Saul Alinsky. "We will see it when we believe it."[12]

Afterword

Bill Bradley

It would be easy, recalling Paul Wellstone, to think only of endings. The plane crash that killed Paul, his wife Sheila, his daughter Marcia, and his staff members Will McLaughlin, Tom Lapic, and Mary McEvoy, ended six remarkable lives and Paul's booming political career. The end seemed especially unfair not just because they were all too young, but because Paul looked to be on the cusp of winning another term in the Senate, where he was becoming steadily more effective even as he remained the institution's conscience. Paul had achieved much; greater things awaited him.

Paul and Sheila were close friends to me and my wife Ernestine. Like so many of their friends, and so many citizens who felt as if they knew the Wellstones personally, I miss them. Paul was an incredibly courageous man. He was a tremendous fighter for what he believed in, and he displayed the courage of his convictions every day. He was extremely bright, and his heart was as big as his mind. Sheila was smart, compassionate, very funny, and saturated with common sense. It can be tempting to remember only their loss.

Paul was indeed one of a kind, and he can't be replaced. But it would be wrong to think his work—or his effectiveness—ended with his life. On the contrary, now that he is gone, we can see more clearly how effective he really was. Paul was best known, I think, for taking principled but sometimes unpopular decisions, such as his votes against welfare reform and the Iraq war. But he was not quixotic. He didn't want to be a noble loser; he wanted to make a real, practical difference. In the end, he did. And the reason he did was because of two particularly crucial talents: he *inspired,* and he *organized.*

Let me speak first about his ability to inspire. Anyone who heard Paul deliver a speech recognized it instantly. He was more than a terrific speaker; he was a real orator. This is an age when many people disrespect old-fashioned oratory, but those who heard Paul understood that great speeches still matter. I learned that lesson well when I ran for president in 2000. Paul often introduced me at campaign stops, and I'd stand off-stage watching as he gave incredibly powerful speeches. He stormed the stage, waving his arms, stirring the crowd with crescendo after crescendo after crescendo, talking passionately about me, about the campaign, and about Americans' highest ideals.

Now, I am not an orator but I could do a fair impersonation of Paul. When I came on stage I would wave my arms and jump up and down in imitation. Beneath the joking, however, I felt deep admiration for his ability. He had a natural gift for public speaking, which he'd developed through relentless practice, and it was through this astounding oratory that he was most inspiring.

Yet his fiery stage presence would have been no more than just a performance if it weren't absolutely authentic. History is cluttered with charismatic leaders who, when viewed up close, disillusion and disappoint. Not Paul. What you saw of him was what he was. If his speeches were inspiring his integrity was even more so.

Paul was driven by and faithful to his principles. He believed deeply in the democratic process, and he was confident that he could make the world a better place. When Paul roared about justice, opportunity, and his hopes for ordinary people, he was voicing his deepest convictions. He learned that in the Senate you never get 100 percent of what you want. He learned how to compromise when he had to, and his ability to compromise made him more effective. But if he sometimes compromised, he never capitulated. He never lost his ability to make a stand. He would vote alone or with just a handful of colleagues—his courageous, prescient opposition to the Iraq war is the best example—because there were certain principles he simply would not compromise. His devotion to his ideals was a challenge and inspiration to the rest of us. In his determination to make the world a better place, he made the Senate a better place.

Paul moved people both through what he said and who he was. He challenged people to work for a better world, and to strive to improve themselves. The legacy of this inspiration is immeasurable. Literally thousands of people have followed Paul's lead by joining the fight for what they believe. The author of this book is one of those people. Bill Lofy began working for Paul during Paul's first term in the Senate. That experience led him to involvement in other political campaigns, to a two-year stint in the Peace Corps, to a graduate degree in public policy, and most recently to a position with Wellstone Action, the nonprofit organization that carries Paul's agenda forward. Paul inspired more than his share of such stories.

Sometimes, during his speeches, when Paul had worked the crowd into a whirl of passion, thrilling them with his descriptions of the work he hoped to do and the people he hoped to help, he would ask, "How are we going to achieve these things?" He supplied the answer with the crescendo: "We're going to organize! We're going to organize! We're going to organize!" His audience would cheer wildly. Leave it to Paul to get hundreds of people wild about the idea of stuffing envelopes, knocking on doors, hosting meetings in their living rooms, and phoning potential supporters. But he did it, and it worked. Those low budget, grassroots Senate campaigns showed that in a world dominated by big money and big media, you can still win by doing what they did 200 years ago—organizing.

This was the second of Paul's most important talents. He knew how to organize. Organizing is much less glamorous than giving speeches, but few people recognize how critical it was to Paul's success. Without an organization to build on, Paul's inspiring speeches would have led nowhere. Imagine rallying an audience as Paul could, but then failing to show them what they can do next. All that energy would be squandered. Or worse, people could end up feeling helpless because there seems to be no way for them to join the process.

But Paul knew how to turn inspiration into action. He built one of the strongest grassroots political movements in the country in the run-up to his first campaign. What's more, Paul built an "organization" strong enough to outlast him. Many movements with charismatic, energetic founders disintegrate once the leader is gone. But the one Paul built remains sturdy even after his death.

After his death, Paul's sons David and Mark, along with

some of Paul's closest friends and advisors, established Well-stone Action. Wellstone Action's mission is to spread Paul's lessons about political leadership. In the process, it has sustained and expanded the grassroots organization Paul established. The core activity of Wellstone Action is called Camp Wellstone, a three-day training program that gives participants practical political skills. It shows them how to build a message and an organization, and how to get elected. Business is thriving. 100,000 people have joined Wellstone Action as members. Some 7,500 people have graduated from Camp Wellstone workshops. A few of them have gone on to run for office themselves—in the 2004 election, 22 Wellstone grads won elections. There are also Campus Camp Wellstones for college students, and a sister organization, the Sheila Wellstone Institute, which advocates for the prevention of domestic violence.

Paul's ongoing presence can be felt at these camps right from the first lesson, which is that a candidate's message must arise from his or her deepest values. All the tricks of the organizing trade—the fundraising, the volunteer efforts, the advertising, and all the rest—mean nothing if they don't flow from the kind of conviction, integrity, and courage that made Paul the leader he was. This is the kind of organizing that would have made Paul proud. It's also the kind of organizing that works.

I am writing this afterword in the spring of 2005, at a time when Democrats have lost the House, the Senate, and the White House. There is much talk, these days, about how to invigorate the Democratic Party and how to win major elections. Whether the party experiences success or more frustration in the short term, we would do well in the long term to look to Paul Wellstone's courageous stands and from-the-ground-up organizing for guidance.

Paul was a great speaker, but his passionate integrity was even more inspiring. Most of all, he did something with all that energy and faith. He did the hard work of organizing voters so that they really could participate in democracy and change the world. Now his protégés have picked up the torch, and they're organizing and inspiring people themselves.

The fact that Paul Wellstone, a short, feisty political science professor from a small Minnesota town, would seriously consider running for U.S. Senate speaks volumes about his deep faith in America and the democratic process. That he won is a testament to his awesome talents. The persistence of Paul's vision even after his death is his great gift to our nation, and his legacy for those of us who counted him as a friend.

Selected
Speeches

Auditor's Race: Endorsement Speech
at DFL Convention
June 5, 1982

Wellstone ran for State Auditor in 1982. It was an office for which he later admitted he was unqualified, but his nominating speech to the DFL convention was a rousing success and solidified Wellstone's reputation as a powerful orator.

I SEEK YOUR endorsement to run as the Democratic Farmer Labor candidate for State Auditor, one of Minnesota's six elected state offices, because I love my country and I love my state and I am worried about our survival— our economic survival in the face of the threat of nuclear war.

Many of the people I have worked with in Minnesota over the years—low and moderate income people, farmers, workers, senior citizens, teachers, students—are now fighting for their economic survival. What the Republican Party wants people to believe is that the most pressing issues of their lives, the economic pain they feel, has nothing to do with politics. That their problems are beyond the reach of government, that there is nothing that the government can or should do. This is a fine philosophy if you own your own big corporation or if you happen to be wealthy

In our campaign in this year of 1982 we are going to speak directly to the issue of fairness. We are going to ask the question: Who Sacrifices, Who Benefits, Who Decides in America today, in Minnesota today?

Who decides to raise the interest rates and whose farm goes under the auctioneer's hammer?

Who decides to subsidize giant corporations while small businesses fold?

Who decides to fight inflation with unemployment, and who is out of work?

Who decides that a safe workplace is too expensive, and who has to risk working there?

Who decides to abandon our central city neighborhoods, and where do these decision makers live?

Who decides to cut job training, housing, and health care programs, and which families suffer?

Who decides to cut taxes for corporations and the wealthy, and what happens to small businesses and the rest of us?

The many should not have to suffer so that a few can prosper. The Republican Party, which ran on the bread and butter issue in 1980, has taken away the bread and butter. Some people are very generous with other people's suffering.

In the 1930's and the 1960's our grandparents, our parents, many of us struggled to make this a better country for the people. Through democracy we gained protection against strike-breaking, through democracy we gained protection against an unsafe workplace, through democracy we gained protection against the ravaging of our air and water, through democracy we gained protection against discrimination by race and sex, through democracy we gained some protection against the terror of unemployment which made people have to take any job under any conditions.

It is democracy itself which is under attack by the Republican Party today. Overnight they are trying to take away fifty years of people's history and they will take more this year, and more the next year, unless we, as the Party of the people, make it clear that this is our history, our country, our state, and we will reassert democratic control.

We believe in democracy. We believe that government can respond to people's needs. We believe that public policy can be based on the policy of fairness. We believe that full employment is the key to social and economic justice, the key to a successful economy and a successful society. But, we do not believe that any of this can be accomplished unless we are involved in the goal-setting that is the essence of democracy.

I am running for state auditor because as a member of the DFL team I will be able to put into effect policies that reflect these democratic values.

As state auditor, I will support productive investment of Minnesota's pension fund. We can and we should, and we must invest some of our pension money, our hard earned capital back into critical sectors of our economy—small farms, businesses, alternative energy and housing programs. This is a small investment that will give us a high rate of return and will help rebuild the economy of our communities and our state. And, this investment must be based on a democratic decision making structure. Our state and local employees must have representation on the state board of investment. It is their money we invest and they have the democratic right to fair representation.

As state auditor I also support ethical divestment.

As state auditor I will support strong labor and strong farm programs that help build our communities. I support a state run workers compensation program because it will assure solid compensation to workers and help bring down costs for small businesses. I support plant closings legislation. Our communities and working people have given many concessions to corporations over the years. This is a question of responsibility. Corporations cannot just leave our communities high and dry without adequate advance notice and some fair compensation.

As state auditor, in these times of rock bottom parity prices for farmers and record high unemployment I will support immediate moratorium on all foreclosures, farm and non-farm. Farmers who have worked hard all their lives should not be thrown off their land and workers who are out of work, no fault of their own, must not be thrown off of their homes. Their loss will be our common loss and we must act now.

As state auditor, I will make assistance to local governments a top priority and will be a strong advocate of citizen participation, and make every effort possible to demystify the financial situation. I believe the auditor can play a key role in helping to bring together local government concerns with state legislative and executive priorities.

As state auditor, I will speak out to provide leadership on critical national issues. The Republicans say that you as a state official have no business talking about the nuclear arms race—it is a national issue. I say that letting Washington make decisions is the prescription for a continued arms race, which is leading to nuclear war. *The survival of Minnesotans is a Minnesota issue.* What the nuclear freeze campaign is showing is that people at the local level can make a difference on this supposedly national issue and as a state official I will support and be a part of this movement for survival.

We must redefine national security to make the security of local communities a priority national goal. National security has little meaning if we have communities without jobs, if food, housing, heat or transportation are not available or affordable, if we cannot provide a good education for our children.

I've traveled around Minnesota and met hundreds of people who are struggling—struggling to keep their jobs, struggling to keep their small businesses, struggling to keep their family farms. They are telling us something. There has never been as great a need for a strong democratic farmer labor party. We have a historical role to play.

We are going to endorse the strongest candidates, we are going to sweep into office in this election year of 1982, we are going to change the politics of Minnesota and in changing the politics of Minnesota we are going to lead the way into changing the way of politics in America: Reclaim low interest rates, reclaim jobs for the unemployed, reclaim affordable housing, reclaim senior rights, reclaim affordable energy, reclaim farms for our family farmers, reclaim education for our children, reclaim a vision of a good society, reclaim the government for the people, less victimization by race, less victimization by sex, less victimization by age, less victimization by income, less victimization by region. Not a heaven on earth but a better earth on earth.

I'd be proud to have your support tonight. I'd be proud to have your support this summer and fall. I'd be proud to have your support in the years to come. Thank you.

U.S. Senate Campaign Stump Speech
Early 1990

Wellstone handwrote his stump speeches in 1990, including this speech delivered to DFL delegates.

I LOVE TO campaign and I can't wait to get started on this campaign against Rudy Boschwitz. I am not worried about his money, or his image-makers and pollsters. We'll raise the money we need to win and we also have some powerful weapons Boschwitz can't begin to match. We have the people working with us, we have the organization, we have the energy, excitement and integrity, we have the issues and conviction to fight for what we care about.

I promise you a fighting, progressive-populist, grasssroots campaign in the Hubert Humphrey—Harry Truman tradition. A campaign that will offer the people of Minnesota a clear alternative to Rudy Boschwitz. A campaign that will be rooted in the participation of people in every city, town, county and district in Minnesota, a campaign that will restore people's faith in politics, a campaign that will light a prairie fire that will sweep Rudy Boschwitz and all his money and wealthy benefactors out of Washington like a pack of grasshoppers. We will win this race!

We must win for health care. My mother Minnie Wellstone is 89 years old, a cafeteria worker, she never made much money. Now she has Alzheimers' disease and is in a nursing home in Northfield. All her resources will have to be depleted until she is eligible for any financial assistance. There is no dignity to such a system. We can do better than that. With your endorsement I'll beat Rudy Boschwitz and lead the fight in the U.S. Senate for universal health care coverage. It is an idea whose time has come. We must provide humane, dignified and affordable health care for all the people in our country.

We must win for our children. One-quarter of our children are poor; one-half of children of color are poor. Every day 100,000 children are homeless. A society that abandons its children with inadequate health care, child-care, education and nutrition is a society that has failed in its mission. We can do better than that. When I am in the United States Senate I will be a strong voice for children, not my children, not your children, but for all the children. We need a New Deal for the children in America.

We must win for the working people. This decade of the 80's—a decade of plants closed, strikes defeated, higher taxes for working people, unions busted, wages depressed, health care and pension benefits cut, broken dreams, broken lives, broken families. It has to stop. When elected to the Senate I'll lead the fight for legislation banning companies from hiring permanent replacements during a strike. It is time to put the government back on the side of the people, not on the side of union busting corporations.

We must win to save the environment. We cannot continue to poison our air, land and water. We must make peace with the planet Earth. Rudy is an election year environmentalist. He is the Senator from Exxon. He takes money from almost every major polluter in the country. We've got to get him out of there and elect a Senator who really cares about the environment. Rudy Boschwitz is the Senator from Exxon; I am going to be the environmentalist Senator from Minnesota, from now on.

Boschwitz says we don't have the money to deal with education, child-care, health care, the environment. He is willing to spend $500 billion to bail out the S and L's and $300 billion dollars a year for the Pentagon. I say we will have no real national security unless we invest in our people, our communities, our economy. I say we will have no real national security unless we invest in the skills, intellect, health and character of our children.

You know where I stand on the issues the vast majority of Minnesotans believe in. I am pro-choice. I am an advocate for children. I stand with working people. I am passionate about fighting for family farmers and rural people. I want my own children to have a future as family farmers and stewards of the land. I believe in businesses that make productive investments in our communities and our economy. I support civil rights and human rights in our country and abroad. I am opposed to discrimination against any group of people. I've struggled with and been inspired by people with disabilities

With the kind of campaign we can wage, I know that Rudy Boschwitz can be beaten this year. But to do it I must have your strong endorsement today. If you believe in what I stand for, and I know that you do, then this time, work for what you believe in and stand with me.

I am a teacher, fighter for children, an environmentalist, a husband and a father. And I am proud to be a Democratic-Farmer-Laborite. What I've stood for, what I have acted on is the heart and soul of our party and the very essence of what Minnesotans believe in.

If Not Now, When? America's Unfinished Agenda
SWARTHMORE COLLEGE
May 31, 1998

Wellstone regularly visited high schools and colleges, and frequently delivered commencement addresses. The following speech was delivered at Swarthmore College's 1998 commencement ceremony.

I THOUGHT I would start out on a personal note. My father was born in the Ukraine, and his family tried to stay one step ahead of the Pogroms, and they moved. He lived in Russia and he fled the country when he was seventeen. When my Dad passed away, my wife, Sheila, and I and our family gave a contribution to an organization called Jewish Fund For Justice and we received a poster that I have both in our home and in my office with a quote from Albert Einstein in which Einstein says, "the pursuit of knowledge for its own sake, the almost passionate love for justice, the strong desire for personal independence, these are features of the Jewish tradition that make me thank my lucky stars I belong to it." I think that there's a little bit of plagiarism in that quote and when the American Friends Service talks about God's spirit implanted in the soul of each person and the dignity and the worth of each person and I think about Swarthmore's mission and this college's commitment to peace and justice in our world and in our country, it makes me especially proud to be here.

On that note, I want to talk very briefly about James Hormel, who graduated from Swarthmore, and is a member of the Board of Governors, Board of Regents. His career has been distinguished by public service, law, philanthropy, business, and community service. He is now up to be ambassador to Luxembourg, but his nomination is blocked in the United States Senate. I have come to the floor several times to say that there has to be a vote. I have looked at his qualifications. I have looked at his record of distinguished service to our country. I've looked at someone who's been a caring father and grandpa, brother and sister, a member of our country, a member of our community. And I cannot see any reason why he's being blocked except maybe for the fact that he is gay. So, in the spirit of the history of Swarthmore

College, in your tradition of justice, of the dignity of each and every person, I'm going to be remembering this college when we have a debate on James Hormel's nomination to be ambassador to Luxembourg because we have to confront this poison politics and we have to end this kind of discrimination in this nation.

To the students, I've been thinking about the kind of advice, since you've given me this chance, that I'd like to give to you. I think that the best thing that I ever said to students at Carleton—and I taught over twenty year—was this: you will be more credible to yourselves and therefore more credible to others if you do not separate the lives that you live from the words that you speak. I do not come here today to tell you what to think, you'd probably run me out of here if I tried to. But I do believe that it is really important to think about not just how to make a living, but, as Ella Baker, who was a great civil rights activist, used to say, about how to make a life. And I would say to you that if you can take some time away from loved ones and away from family—and I would never want you to make your loved ones casualties of your community activism—but if you can take some time away from loved ones, some time away from family, and give it to the community, give it to our country, give it to our world, I think you will make a huge difference, an enormous difference, and I hope you will do that. I think that is so much a part of Swarthmore College's tradition.

At a lot of gatherings like this I worry because, as students are about to graduate, people will come and they will speak and they will say, "now that you've graduated from Swarthmore or Carleton or the University of Minnesota or any school you have the tools to go out there and compete in the economy and do well." I don't come here today to tell you not to do well, but I think that if you were to think for a moment about how you got to this point of enormous accomplishment, I don't think that the word would be independence, I think the key word would be interdependence. Think of parents, think of family, think of relationships with other students, think of friendships, think of the bond that so many of you have with one another. And so I raise this question, why not in our country? Why not the same focus on the ways that we are interdependent? Why not the same focus on relationships? On how to treat one another. Why not define a community where we all do better—when we all do better? I think that that's the direction our country needs to go.

I bring a reading here today, to Swarthmore. It was taken from a book that was just published. The title, "*Make Gentle the Life of this World: The Vision of Robert F. Kennedy.*" It was sent to me by one of his sons, Max Kennedy, who now lives in Boston. I quote from Robert Kennedy. This was a speech that Bobby Kennedy gave March 18, 1968 to students at Kansas University. And I quote, "The gross national product does not allow for the health of our children; the quality of their education; or the joy of their play. It does not include the beauty of our poetry or the strength of our marriages, the intelligence of our public debate, or the intelligence or integrity of our public officials. It measures neither wit nor courage. Neither our vision, our wisdom, or our learning. Neither our compassion nor devotion to our country. It measures everything, in short, except that which makes life worthwhile. And it can tell us everything about America except why we are proud that we are Americans."

We can do much better as a country. We should not focus just on how to grow our economy, but we should focus on how we can grow the quality of our lives, and how we can grow the quality of our life as a nation. We must foster a new atmosphere where values become sensitive to public policy. And we must build a nation, a community where no person, no neighborhood, and no community feels left behind.

I come here today to pose a question for you at this baccalaureate, and this is my question. How can it be that in the United States of America, today, at the peek of our economic performance, we are still being told that we cannot provide a good education for every child? We are still being told that we cannot provide good health care for every citizen. We are still being told that people can't look forward to jobs that they can support themselves and their children on. We're still being told that we cannot achieve the goal of having every five-year old come to kindergarten ready to learn, knowing the alphabet, knowing how to spell her name, knowing colors, shapes, and sizes, having been read to widely with that wonderful readiness to learn. How can it be that we are being told that we cannot do this at the peak of our economic performance? I say to you today that it is not right. It is not acceptable. We can do much better, and if not now, when? If we don't do this now, when will we do it as a nation?

On Friday, on my way back from Minnesota, I went down to the Mississippi Delta. I had been there a year earlier, and I had promised to come back. I was at a community gathering with an African-American teacher, Robert Hall, who probably makes twenty-two to twenty-three thousand dollars a year. Incredibly dedicated teacher. He stood up at a community meeting, and he said, "Senator"—this was June, a year ago—"It's hard to give the students hope. Only half our students graduate. Would you come back for graduation?" And then, their graduation, as it turns out, is the same day, Sunday, today. So I asked him if I could come Friday, to teach. I was a teacher, and so I came to speak at the high school. I got off the plane and I was met at the airport, and as we were driving to Tunica, Mississippi, a man said to me, "First we're going to go to the elementary school and you will address the third and fourth graders on the last day of class."

I said, "Address? On the last day of school?" But I said okay, and we went there. I'll address them, I'm a teacher. I said, do you like school? Do you like education? What's important about it? And one young girl said, "It's important because I can be what I want to be." And I said, well what do you want to be? And there were forty hands up, and the rest of the hour was students talking about what they want to be. One of them wanted to be a psychiatrist. I thought that was interesting. Or a doctor. Or a professional wrestler. Or a professional basketball player. Or a teacher. Or an artist. Or a business person, on and on and on. Those children had hope.

I will tell you here today at Swarthmore,—because of how much I think of the college, and because I was a teacher and I'll be a teacher again—I saw at Carleton College how, if you take that spark of learning that those children have, and you ignite it, you can take a child from any background to a lifetime of creativity and accomplishment. But if you pour cold water on that spark of learning, it is the cruelest and most short sighted thing we can do as a nation. We pour cold water on that spark of learning for too many children. Another question I pose, and I'm going to keep asking this question and asking this question, keep pressing this with this question. How can it be in a country I love so much, and a country that's doing so well economically, a country at the peak of its economic performance, that one out of every four children under the age of three is growing up poor in America? One out of every two children of color under the age of three is growing up poor in America. We have a set of social arrangements in our country that allow children to be the most poverty stricken group.

That is a betrayal of our heritage. The impoverishment of so many children is our national disgrace. Carol mentioned that I traveled some last year. I started out in the Mississippi Delta, not to come in to tell people what to do, not to be presumptuous, not to be pretentious. I know better than that. But I wanted to go there because I had read a book by Nick Kotz, who had won a Pulitzer prize for his book, *Let Them Eat Promises*. I used to assign it to students. And he described the visit where Bobby Kennedy came and some of you will probably remember this. And he was focused on hunger, and there was a little African-American boy, and Bobby Kennedy was trying to play with him, but the little boy couldn't respond. He just had a vacant look. He was so severely malnourished. And Bobby Kennedy kept trying to play with him like we do with our children and grandchildren, but the little boy didn't respond. And then Bobby Kennedy broke down crying.

I wanted to start our trip in a neighborhood in the Mississippi Delta. And then we went to East L.A., and then we went to Chicago in the Pilsen neighborhood, a Latino community, and then public housing projects—the Robert Taylor Homes and Ida Wells. And then we went to inner-city Baltimore, and then we went to Appalachia. I can tell you that we met a lot of heroines and heroes who give lie to the argument that nothing can be done. If I had the hours, I would celebrate their worth. We can do so much at the community level if people have the resources. But I also want to tell you that everywhere we went, what people were saying, citizens in our country, what they were saying was, "what happened to our national vow, our vow as a nation, that there should be equal opportunity for every child? Not in our community. And where are the jobs or the business opportunities so that we can do well economically and we can give our children the care we know they need and deserve?" That's what we heard. And then we traveled to other parts of our country, and when we did, it was the same kind of issues.

And I will summarize, in a different voice, "Senator, my daughter is twenty-four. She graduated from college. She's a diabetic. She now will be off our health insurance plan. I know that the insurance companies are no longer allowed to deny her coverage, but it's going to cost her ten thousand dollars a year, and she won't be able to afford it."

"Senator, I want you to meet my husband Joe. You met him a year ago. I told you he only had two months to live, but he's a fighter. Joe's now in a wheelchair. He's a fighter. Please come over and say hello." And so I did. And then she takes me aside and she says, "Every day it's a nightmare. I'm on the phone battling with some of these insurance companies because I don't know what they'll cover."

I don't think any American, with a loved one struggling with an illness, cancer, or otherwise, should have to worry about whether or not there'll be decent care, should have to be battling for coverage every day.

Or, "Senator, I'm a student at Moorhead State University in Minnesota. It's taken me six years to graduate. I've been working for forty hours a week for the last six years."

Or, "Senator, I sell plasma at the beginning of the semester in order to be able to buy textbooks."

Or, "Senator, I'm a single parent. I'm one of the welfare mothers you hear about, but I'm in the community college. I want to be independent, but now I'm being told, in the name of welfare reform, that I have to leave school and take a job, but the job pays six dollars and fifty cents an hour and I won't have health care in a year and I'll be worse off. Please let me finish my schooling, my education, so I can support my children."

Or, "Senator, we're both thirty, our combined income is thirty-five thousand dollars a year, but it costs us twelve thousand dollars in child care for our two children."

Can't we do better?

Or, "Senator, my dad is a Vietnam vet. He took a shower last week, but when he came out of the shower he wouldn't talk to anybody any longer. We're told that he suffers from post traumatic stress syndrome. But we don't have any compensation, how do we get him the care?"

I don't think politics has anything to do with the left, right, or center. It has to do with trying to do well for people. And the other thing, and I get to say this to you, the graduating seniors that are here, and I'm sure parents and family may very well agree with this sentiment. "Senator, we're disillusioned by politics, we think both parties are run by the same investors, we don't have any faith any longer, we think the special interests dominate the process, we have so little confidence in politics, and we don't think politics is very important." A friend who teaches at the Kennedy at Harvard said he had a seminar with students last week and he was talking about electoral politics and he was talking about a campaign in which he was involved in New Hampshire, in 1966 with Eugene McCarthy, from Minnesota. The students said, "Yeah, but that's when politics were important."

I want to say today, to the students that I know how many of you have been involved in community service—that is so important. My worry is when people say community service is good but involvement in politics is unsavory. We need you. We need you involved in community service, we need you to be the really great teachers of the future, we need you involved in community service, we need you to be mentors and tutors—and many of you have been—and to help children and families battle the odds. We need you to volunteer at community health care clinics, and above and beyond whatever you do during your work days, we need you as business people and lawyers to do community work. But we also need you to care about public policy, to be the citizens speaking out for better public policy and more integrity in politics, and for you to believe that government and public policy can make a difference. That politics is not just about power and money games, politics can be about the improvement of people's lives, about lessening human suffering in our world and bringing about more peace and more justice.

And I say to you students at Swarthmore, as a political scientist and a United States Senator, that in the last analysis, politics is what we create, by what we do, by what we hope for, by what we dare to imagine.

Here's what I dare to imagine. I think this is very much in the American Friends Service tradition. As a United States Senator from Minnesota, I dare to imagine, as a father and now a grandfather of three, I dare to imagine a country, where I travel, and meet children, and I pick up an infant and hold her in my arms, I want to be able to believe, that in the United States of America, I dare to imagine a country where every child I hold in my hands, are all God's children, regardless of the color of their skin, regardless of whether they're boy or girl, regardless of religion, regardless of rich or poor, regardless of urban or rural, that every child I hold in my hands, will have the same chance to reach her full potential or his full potential. That is the goodness of our country. That is the American dream.

In closing, to the graduating seniors, I say this with all sincerity. I do not believe the future will belong to those who are content with the present, I do not believe the future will belong to the cynics, or to those who stand on the side-line. The future will belong to those who have passion, and to those who are willing to make the personal commitment to make our country better. The future will belong to those who believe in the beauty of their dreams.

Notes

CHAPTER I

1. CNN Wolf Blitzer Reports, October 25, 2002, transcript, http://www.cgi.cnn.com/TRANSCRIPTS/0210/25/wbr.00.html.

2. The tributes to Wellstone are from the following: John Nichols, "Paul Wellstone: An Appreciation," The Nation Online, October 25, 2002, http://www.thenation.com/doc.mhtml%3Fi=20021111&s=nichols3; Liza Porteus, "Lawmakers Remember Wellstone," http://www.foxnews.com/story/0,2933,66724,00.html; Paul Krugman, "For the People," New York Times, October 29, 2002, A31; John Miller, "Paul Wellstone, RIP," National Review Online, October 25, 2002, http://www.nationalreview.com/miller/miller102502a.asp; Robert Novak, "Left-Wing Prof Loved the Game," Chicago Sun-Times, October 28, 2002, 35; Jill Zuckman, "Senate Loses 'Gallant' Voice of Liberals," Chicago Tribune, October 26, 2002.

3. "A Star's Crash Landing," Newsweek, March 25, 1991, 39; Leslie Phillips, "Blunt Minnesota Senator Pays Price," USA Today, March 18, 1991, 3A; Edward Walsh, "Wellstone Faces Fallout of Anti-War Offensive," Washington Post, April 7, 1991, A1; Lynn Rosellini, "Under the Senate's Skin," U.S. News and World Report, June 24, 1991.

4. Walsh, "Wellstone Faces Fallout of Anti-War Offensive," *Washington Post*, April 7, 1991.

5. Richard Berke, "The Education of Paul Wellstone," *New York Times Magazine*, November 10, 1991, 36.

CHAPTER 2

1. Ed Henry, "Wellstone Was Son of 'Washington Nobody,'" *Washingtonian Magazine*, December 2002, 11.

2. Dennis J. McGrath and Dane Smith, *Professor Wellstone Goes to Washington: The Inside Story of a Grassroots U.S. Senate Campaign* (Minneapolis: University of Minnesota Press, 1995), 22.

3. Hardworking Pictures, Eleanor Fullerton interview transcript. All quotations from Eleanor Fullerton interview transcript did not appear in the *Wellstone!* documentary itself.

4. Essay found in Wellstone's personal papers.

5. McGrath and Smith, *Professor Wellstone Goes to Washington*, 26.

6. Henry, "Wellstone Was Son of 'Washington Nobody,'" 11.

7. Paul Wellstone, *The Conscience of a Liberal: Reclaiming the Compassionate Agenda* (New York: Random House, 2001), 30.

8. Hardworking Pictures, Fullerton interview transcript.

9. Wellstone, *Conscience of a Liberal*, 30.

10. Transcript of on-camera interview of Wellstone, produced in 1990 by his campaign staff.

11. Hardworking Pictures, Fullerton interview transcript.

12. Hardworking Pictures, Fullerton interview transcript.

13. Hardworking Pictures, Fullerton interview transcript.

14. Mordecai Specktor, "My Breakfast with Paul Wellstone," *American Jewish World of Minnesota,* October 30, 2003, available at http://www.interfaithfamily.com/article/issue97/specktor.phtml.

15. Specktor, "My Breakfast With Paul Wellstone."

16. Wellstone, *Conscience of a Liberal*, 55.

17. Wellstone, *Conscience of a Liberal*, 56.

18. Hardworking Pictures, Fullerton interview transcript.

19. McGrath and Smith, *Professor Wellstone Goes to Washington*, 24.

20. Found in Wellstone's personal papers.

21. McGrath and Smith, *Professor Wellstone Goes to Washington*, 26.

22. Wellstone, unpublished draft of Wellstone autobiography, taken from the author's personal files, 20.

23. Hardworking Pictures, Bill Lamb interview transcript. All quotations from Bill Lamb interview transcript did not appear in the *Wellstone!* documentary itself.

24. High school report card, from Wellstone's personal papers.

25. From Leon Wellstone's writings, taken from Paul Wellstone's personal papers.

26. Wellstone, *Conscience of a Liberal*, 31.

27. Transcript of on-camera interview of Wellstone, produced in 1990 by his campaign staff.

28. Transcript of on-camera interview of Wellstone, produced in 1990 by his campaign staff.

29. Transcript of on-camera interview of Wellstone, produced in 1990 by his campaign staff.

30. From Leon Wellstone's writings, taken from Paul Wellstone's personal papers.

31. Hardworking Pictures, Fullerton interview transcript.

32. From Leon Wellstone's writings, taken from Paul Wellstone's personal papers.

33. Hardworking Pictures, Dianne Stimson interview transcript. All quotations from Dianne Stimson interview transcript did not appear in the *Wellstone!* documentary itself.

34. Hardworking Pictures, Sam Kaplan interview transcript. All quotations from Sam Kaplan interview transcript did not appear in the *Wellstone!* documentary itself.

35. Hardworking Pictures, Stimson interview transcript.

36. Transcript of on-camera interview of Wellstone, produced in 1990 by his campaign staff.

37. Hardworking Pictures, Lamb interview transcript.

38. Hardworking Pictures, Fullerton interview transcript.

39. Transcript of on-camera interview of Wellstone, produced in 1990 by his campaign staff.

40. Hardworking Pictures, Stimson interview transcript.

41. Hardworking Pictures, Stimson interview transcript.

42. Paul Wellstone, "Black Militants in the Ghetto: Why They Resort to Violence" (Ph.D. dissertation, University of North Carolina, 1969).

43. Hardworking Pictures, Stimson interview transcript.

44. Wellstone, "Black Militants in the Ghetto."

45. David Schwartz, "U.S. Senate Gains a Controversial Voice," *Carolina Alumni Review* (summer 1991): 29.

46. Transcript of on-camera interview of Wellstone, produced in 1990 by his campaign staff.

47. John Nichols, "Portrait of a Founder," available at http://www.progressive.org/nichols9901.htm.

48. Hardworking Pictures, Walter Mondale interview transcript. All quotations from Walter Mondale interview transcript did not appear in the *Wellstone!* documentary itself.

49. Nichols, "Portrait of a Founder."

50. Transcript of on-camera interview of Wellstone, produced in 1990 by his campaign staff.

51. Jonathan Lange, "Senator's Disciples Carry on His Work," *Baltimore Sun*, November 4, 2002.

52. Tom Bartel, "Wellstone the Teacher," *The Rake*, November 2002.

53. "Senator Paul Wellstone Killed in Plane Crash," *St. Paul Pioneer Press*, October 25, 2002, available at http://www.twincities.com/mld/pioneerpress/4368592.htm.

54. Wellstone, *Conscience of a Liberal*, 5.

55. Saul Alinsky, *Rules for Radicals* (New York: Random House, 1971).

56. "An Interview with Sen. Paul Wellstone," available at http://www.insidepolitics.org/intwellstone.html

57. Paul Wellstone, *How the Rural Poor Got Power* (Minneapolis: University of Minnesota Press, 2003), viii.

58. Wellstone, *How the Rural Poor Got Power*, 4.

59. Wellstone, *How the Rural Poor Got Power*, 80.

60. Warren Wolfe, "Two-Fisted Group Fights for Poor through Courts," *Minneapolis Tribune*, September 17, 1973.

61. Hardworking Pictures, Patty Fritz interview transcript. All quotations from Patty Fritz interview transcript did not appear in the *Wellstone!* documentary itself.

62. After losing in 2002, Fritz went on to run for state legislature again in 2004 and won. She now represents portions of rural Rice County in the Minnesota House of Representatives.

63. Hardworking Pictures, Kari Moe interview transcript. All quotations from Kari Moe interview transcript did not appear in the *Wellstone!* documentary itself.

64. Wellstone, *How the Rural Poor Got Power*, 223.

CHAPTER 3

1. Mary Losure, "Wellstone Learned to Listen, Lead during Powerline Protests," Minnesota Public Radio, December 9, 2002.

2. Losure, "Wellstone Learned to Listen."

3. Losure, "Wellstone Learned to Listen."

4. Losure, "Wellstone Learned to Listen."

5. Losure, "Wellstone Learned to Listen."

6. Review of *Powerline*, in *Michigan Law Review* 80, no. 4 (1982): 948–52.

7. Katherine Lanpher, "Growing Up Wellstone," *St. Paul Pioneer Press*, January 6, 1991.

8. Lanpher, "Growing Up Wellstone."

9. Transcript of speech, taken from Wellstone's personal papers.

10. Paul Taylor, "What I Meant Was," *Washington Post*, August 29, 1982, A5.

11. Wellstone's diary from 1982 auditor's race, taken from his personal papers.

12. Memo to DFL Party officials, taken from Wellstone's personal papers.

13. McGrath and Smith, *Professor Wellstone Goes to Washington*, 15.

14. Hardworking Pictures, Scott Adams interview transcript. All quotations from Scott Adams interview transcript did not appear in the *Wellstone!* documentary itself.

15. Hardworking Pictures, Adams interview transcript.

16. McGrath and Smith, *Professor Wellstone Goes to Washington*, 12.

17. "The Best of the Twin Cities 1989: Best Speaker," *Mpls.St.Paul Magazine*, January 1989.

18. "Wellstone Talks of Campaigning and Speaking" *The Carletonian* (student newspaper), February 24, 1989.

19. Hardworking Pictures, Adams interview transcript.

20. Hardworking Pictures, Adams interview transcript.

21. McGrath and Smith, *Professor Wellstone Goes to Washington*, 123.

22. McGrath and Smith, *Professor Wellstone Goes to Washington*, 159.

23. Speech transcripts, from Wellstone's personal papers.

24. Hardworking Pictures, Jeff Blodgett interview transcript. All quotations from Jeff Blodgett interview transcript did not appear in the *Wellstone!* documentary itself.

25. Dennis McGrath, "Running Uphill: 8 Weeks Inside the Wellstone Campaign," *Star Tribune*, November 11, 1990.

26. Doug Grow, "Boschwitz's Smiley Face Turns Ugly," *Star Tribune*, November 4, 1990.

27. Tom Hamburger, "Boschwitz Letter Sparks Talk by Jews in U.S., Israel," *Star Tribune*, November 9, 1990.

28. Grow, "Boschwitz's Smiley Face."

29. McGrath and Smith, *Professor Wellstone Goes to Washington*, 258.

CHAPTER 4

1. Mark Brunswick and Rob Hotakainen, "Wellstone's Transition: A Triumph or Sellout?" *Star Tribune*, October 18, 2002, 1A.

2. Josh Tyrangiel, "Death on the Campaign Trail," *Time*, November 4, 2002.

3. Cliff Haas, "Wellstone Keeps Vow to Be Outspoken, Says He Detests Helms," *Star Tribune*, November 16, 1990.

4. John Nichols, "Paul Wellstone, Fighter," *Nation*, May 9, 2002 (available at www.thenation.com/doc.mhtml%Fi=20020527&s=Nichols).

5. Wellstone, unpublished draft of Wellstone autobiography, 121.

6. Donald Mathews, *U.S. Senators and Their World* (Westport, CT: Greenwood Press, 1980).

7. Wellstone, *Conscience of a Liberal*, 158.

8. Hardworking Pictures, Mondale interview transcript.

9. Wellstone, *Conscience of a Liberal*, 162.

10. Author interview with Colin McGinnis, June 13, 2003.

11. Wellstone, unpublished draft of Wellstone autobiography, 183.

12. Hardworking Pictures, Josh Syrjamaki interview transcript. All quotations from Josh Syrjamaki interview transcript did not appear in the *Wellstone!* documentary itself.

13. Jim Klobuchar, "True News Flash: A Politician Keeps a Promise," *Star Tribune*, May 3, 1992, 3B.

14. Klobuchar, "True News Flash."

15. Klobuchar, "True News Flash."

16. Tom Hamburger and Dane Smith, "New Gains by a New Wellstone," *Star Tribune*, January 10, 1993.

17. "The Wellspring of Lobby Reform," *New York Times*, May 7, 1993, A30.

18. Hardworking Pictures, Blodgett interview transcript.

19. Wellstone, *Conscience of a Liberal*, 160.
20. Hardworking Pictures, Syrjamaki interview transcript.
21. Hardworking Pictures, Syrjamaki interview transcript.
22. Hardworking Pictures, Moe interview transcript.
23. Wellstone campaign ad, 1996.
24. Wellstone, unpublished draft, 133.
25. Hardworking Pictures, Mandy Grunwald interview transcript. All quotations from Mandy Grunwald interview transcript did not appear in the *Wellstone!* documentary itself.

CHAPTER 5

1. *Congressional Record*, January 7, 1997.
2. Brunswick and Hotakainen, "Wellstone's Transition."
3. Charles Hurt, "Even Helms Became a Friend," *Charlotte Observer*, October 26, 2002.
4. "President Clinton and Secretary of Labor Alexis M. Herman Applaud Bipartisan Effort to Launch New Job Delivery System," press release from the United States Department of Labor, available at http://www.doleta.gov/usworkforce/archive/press/finalregspress.htm.
5. Deborah Sontag, "When Politics Is Personal," *New York Times Magazine*, September 15, 2002, 90.
6. Sontag, "When Politics Is Personal."
7. Sontag, "When Politics Is Personal."
8. Author interview with McGinnis.
9. Floor speech by Senator Ted Kennedy, October 2002.
10. Floor speech by Senator Byron Dorgan, October 2002.
11. Hardworking Pictures, Stimson interview transcript.
12. Wellstone, unpublished draft of Wellstone autobiography, taken from the author's personal files.
13. Wellstone, unpublished draft of Wellstone autobiography, taken from the author's personal files.
14. Tom Hamburger, "Wellstone One Step Away from Making It Official," *Star Tribune*, December 5, 1998.
15. Dane Smith, "Wellstone: Bad Back Prevents Bid in 2000," *Star Tribune*, January 10, 1999.
16. Lori Sturdevant, "Wellstone Now a Leading Surrogate for Bradley," *Star Tribune*, January 18, 2000.
17. Sturdevant, "Wellstone Now a Leading Surrogate for Bradley."
18. Sturdevant, "Wellstone Now a Leading Surrogate for Bradley."

19. Bob Whereatt, "Wellstone Foresees 2 Busy Terms," *Star Tribune*, November 8, 1990.

CHAPTER 6

1. Bob Whereatt, "Wellstone's Job Approval Is Near Its Previous High; Don't Seek a 3rd Term, Most Say," *Star Tribune*, January 18, 2000.

2. Laura McCallum, "Wellstone Breaks Pledge, Will Run Again," Minnesota Public Radio, January 17, 2001, available at http://news .minnesota.publicradio.org/features/200101/17_mccalluml_wellstone.

3. Dane Smith, "Cheney Advises Pawlenty Not to Run for Senate; Majority Leader Bows to Request from White House," *Star Tribune*, April 19, 2001.

4. Smith, "Cheney Advises Pawlenty Not to Run."

5. Patricia Lopez, "Coleman's Journey Crosses Political Divide," *Star Tribune*, October 16, 2002.

6. Mark Brunswick, "Coleman: I'm 'Prophet of Hope,'" *Star Tribune*, February 12, 2002.

7. Patricia Lopez, "Condemning Corporate Crime; Coleman, Wellstone Have Tug of War over Who Would Be a Better Watchdog," *Star Tribune*, August 21, 2002.

8. Lopez, "Condemning Corporate Crime."

9. Patricia Lopez, "Coleman, Wellstone Camps Argue Defense Issues," *Star Tribune*, September 20, 2002.

10. E-mail from Democratic Senatorial Campaign Committee official to Jeff Blodgett.

11. *Congressional Record*, October 3, 2002.

12. Rob Hotakainen, "Wellstone Says No to Iraq Resolution," *Star Tribune*, October 3, 2002.

13. Hotakainen, "Wellstone Says No."

14. Kevin Diaz, "Bush's Iraq Plan Gets Boost," *Star Tribune*, October 4, 2002.

15. Helen Dewar, "For Wellstone, Iraq Vote Is a Risk but Not a Choice," *Washington Post*, October 9, 2002.

CHAPTER 7

1. Related by Professor Fred Greenstein from a personal conversation with Mathews.

2. Hardworking Pictures, E. J. Dionne interview transcript. All quo-

tations from E. J. Dionne interview transcript did not appear in the *Wellstone!* documentary itself.

3. Hardworking Pictures, Blodgett interview transcript.

4. From Wellstone's personal papers.

5. Hardworking Pictures, Mondale interview transcript.

6. Eric Fure-Slocum, e-mail message to author, Dec. 23, 2004.

7. Hardworking Pictures, Dionne interview transcript.

8. Hardworking Pictures, Senator Mike DeWine interview transcript.

9. Hardworking Pictures, Senator Tim Johnson interview transcript.

10. Hardworking Pictures, Dionne interview transcript.

11. William Wordsworth, "Character of the Happy Warrior," *William Wordsworth: Favorite Poems* (New York: Dover), 50.

12. Alinsky, *Rules for Radicals*, 196.

Text design by Jillian Downey
Typesetting by Delmastype, Ann Arbor, Michigan.
Font: Goudy

Frederic W. Goudy designed Goudy Old Style in 1915,
and many subsequent additions to the typeface family were
created over the next several decades.

—courtesy www.adobe.com